Donna Kooler's
555 Christmas
Cross-Stitch Designs

Donna Kooler's
555 Christmas
Cross-Stitch Designs

Sterling Publishing Co., Inc. New York
A Sterling/Chapelle Book

CHAPELLE LTD.

Owner: Jo Packham
Editor: Karmen Quinney
Staff: Marie Barber, Ann Bear, Areta Bingham,
   Kass Burchett, Rebecca Christensen,
   Dana Durney, Holly Fuller, Marilyn Goff,
   Holly Hollingsworth, Shawn Hsu,
   Susan Jorgensen, Barbara Milburn, Linda Orton,
   Leslie Ridenour, Cindy Stoeckl

KOOLER DESIGN STUDIO

Editor: Priscilla Timm
President: Donna Kooler
Executive Vice President: Linda Gillum
Vice President: Priscilla Timm
Creative Director: Deanna Hall West
Photography Stylists: Donna Kooler, Deanna Hall West
Marketing Director: Loretta Heden
Design Staff: Linda Gillum, Nancy Rossi, Barbara Baatz,
   Jorja Hernandez, Sandy Orton
Contributing Artists: Donna Yuen, Pam Johnson
Staff: Sara Angle, Jennifer Drake, Anita Forfang,
   Virginia Hanley-Rivett, Marsha Hinkson,
   Arlis Johnson, Lori Patton, Char Randolph,
   Giana Shaw
Photography: Dianne Woods; Berkeley, CA.

Library of Congress Cataloging-in-Publication Data

Kooler, Donna.
   Donna Kooler's 555 Christmas cross-stitch designs.
         p.   cm.
   "A Sterling/Chapelle book."
   ISBN 0-8069-2072-6
   1. Cross-stitch—patterns. 2. Christmas decorations.
   I. Title. II. Title: 555 Christmas cross-stitch designs.
   TT778.C76.K666 1999   99-14089
   746.44'304—dc21
            CIP
10 9 8 7 6 5 4 3 2 1

Published by Sterling Publishing Company, Inc.,
387 Park Avenue South, New York, NY 10016
© 1999 by Chapelle Limited
Distributed in Canada by Sterling Publishing
⅀ Canadian Manda Group, One Atlantic Avenue, Suite 105
Toronto, Ontario, Canada M6K 3E7
Distributed in Great Britain and Europe by Cassell PLC
Wellington House, 125 Strand, London WC2R 0BB, England
Distributed in Australia by Capricorn Link (Australia) Pty Ltd.
P.O. Box 6651, Baulkham Hills, Business Centre, NSW 2153,
Australia
Printed in China
All Rights Reserved

Sterling ISBN 0-8069-2072-6

Dedicated to all who make
Christmas bright and beautiful
with the work of their hands.

Donna Kooler

If you have any questions or comments, please contact: Chapelle Ltd., Inc., P.O. Box 9252 Ogden, UT 84409 (801) 621-2777 • FAX (801) 621-2788 • E-mail Chapelle1@ aol.com

Table of Contents

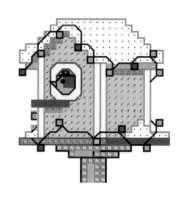

General Instructions

Introduction
Contained in this book are 555 counted cross-stitch Christmas designs. To create one-of-a-kind motifs, vary colors in graphed designs. The codes for samplers are placed following the graphed design.

Fabric for Cross-stitch
Counted cross-stitch is worked on even-weave fabrics. These fabrics are manufactured specifically for counted-thread embroidery, and are woven with the same number of vertical as horizontal threads per inch.

Because the number of threads in the fabric is equal in each direction, each stitch will be the same size. The number of threads per inch in even-weave fabrics determines the size of a finished design.

Number of Strands
The number of strands used per stitch varies, depending on the fabric used. Generally, the rule to follow for cross-stitching is three strands on Aida 11, two strands on Aida 14, one or two strands on Aida 18 (depending on desired thickness of stitches), and one strand on Hardanger 22.

For backstitching, use one strand on all fabrics. When completing a french knot, use two strands and one wrap on all fabrics, unless otherwise directed.

Finished Design Size
To determine the size of the finished design, divide the stitch count by the number of threads per inch of fabric. When design is stitched over two threads, divide stitch count by half the threads per inch. For example, if a design with a stitch count of 120 width and 250 length were stitched on a 28 count linen over two threads, the finished size would be 8⅝" x 17⅞".

Preparing Fabric
Cut fabric at least 3" larger on all sides than the finished design size to ensure enough space for desired assembly. To prevent fraying, whipstitch or machine-zigzag along the raw edges or apply liquid fray preventive.

Needles for Cross-stitch
Blunt needles should slip easily through the fabric holes without piercing fabric threads. For fabric with 11 or fewer threads per inch, use a tapestry needle size 24; for 14 threads per inch, use a tapestry needle size 24 or 26; for 18 or more threads per inch, use a tapestry needle size 26. Never leave the needle in the design area of the fabric. It may leave rust or a permanent impression on the fabric.

Floss
All numbers and color names on the codes represent the DMC brand of floss. Use 18" lengths of floss. For best coverage, separate the strands and dampen with a wet sponge. Then put together the number of strands required for the fabric used.

Centering Design
Fold the fabric in half horizontally, then vertically. Place a pin in the fold point to mark the center. Locate the center of the design on the graph. To help in centering the designs, arrows are provided at left and right-side center and top and bottom center. Begin stitching all designs at the center point of the graph and fabric.

Securing Floss
Insert needle up from the underside of the fabric at starting point. Hold 1" of thread behind the fabric and stitch over it, securing with the first few stitches. To finish thread, run under four or more stitches on the back of the design. Never knot floss, unless working on clothing.

Another method of securing floss is the waste knot. Knot floss and insert needle down from the right top side of the fabric about 1" from design area. Work several stitches over the thread to secure. Cut off the knot later.

Carrying Floss
To carry floss, weave floss under the previously worked stitches on the back. Do not carry thread across any fabric that is not or will not be stitched. Loose threads, especially dark ones, will show through the fabric.

Cleaning Finished Design

When stitching is finished, soak the fabric in cold water with a mild soap for five to ten minutes. Rinse well and roll in a towel to remove excess water. Do not wring. Place the piece face down on a dry towel and iron on a warm setting until the fabric is dry.

Cross-stitch (XS)

Stitches are done in a row or, if necessary, one at a time in an area.

1. Insert needle up between woven threads at A.

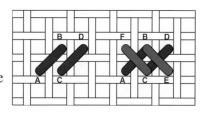

2. Go down at B, the opening diagonally across from A.

3. Come up at C and go down at D, etc.

4. To complete the top stitches creating an "X", come up at E and go down at B, come up at C and go down at F, etc. All top stitches should lie in the same direction.

Backstitch (BS)

1. Insert needle up between woven threads at A.

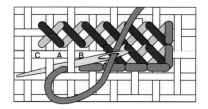

2. Go down at B, one opening to the right.

3. Come up at C.

4. Go down at A, one opening to the right.

French Knot (FK)

1. Insert needle up between woven threads at A, using one strand of embroidery floss.

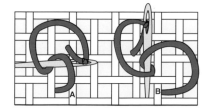

2. Loosely wrap floss once around needle.

3. Go down at B, the opening across from A. Pull floss taut as needle is pushed down through fabric.

4. Carry floss across back of work between knots.

Lazy Daisy Stitch (LD)

1. Insert needle up between woven threads at A.

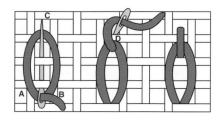

2. Go down at B, using same opening as A.

3. Come up at C, crossing under two threads. Pull through, holding floss under needle to form loop.

4. Go down at D, crossing one thread.

Long Stitch (LS)

1. Insert needle up between woven threads at A.

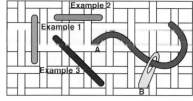

2. Go down at B, crossing two threads. Pull flat. Repeat A–B for each stitch. Stitch may be horizontal, verticle, or diagonal as indicated in examples 1, 2, and 3. The length of the stitch should be the same as the length indicated on the graph.

Half-cross Stitch (HC)

Stitches are done in a row horizontally from the left to the right.

1. Insert needle up between woven threads at A.

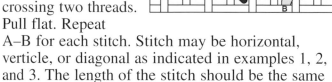

2. Go down at B, the opening diagonally across from A.

3. Come up at C and down at D, etc.

Folk
Art
Christmas

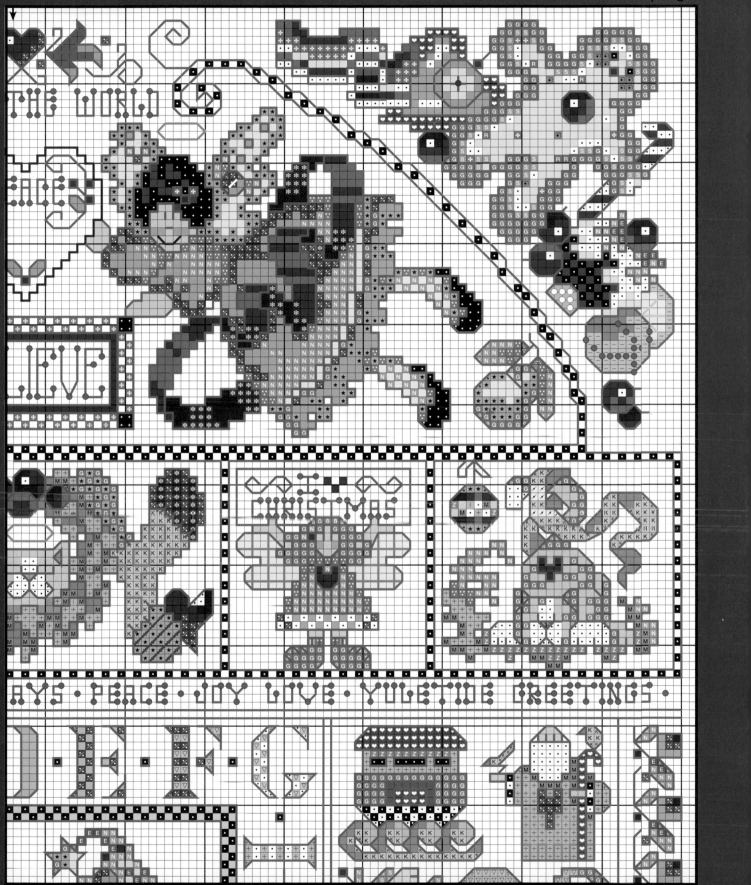

Bottom Left

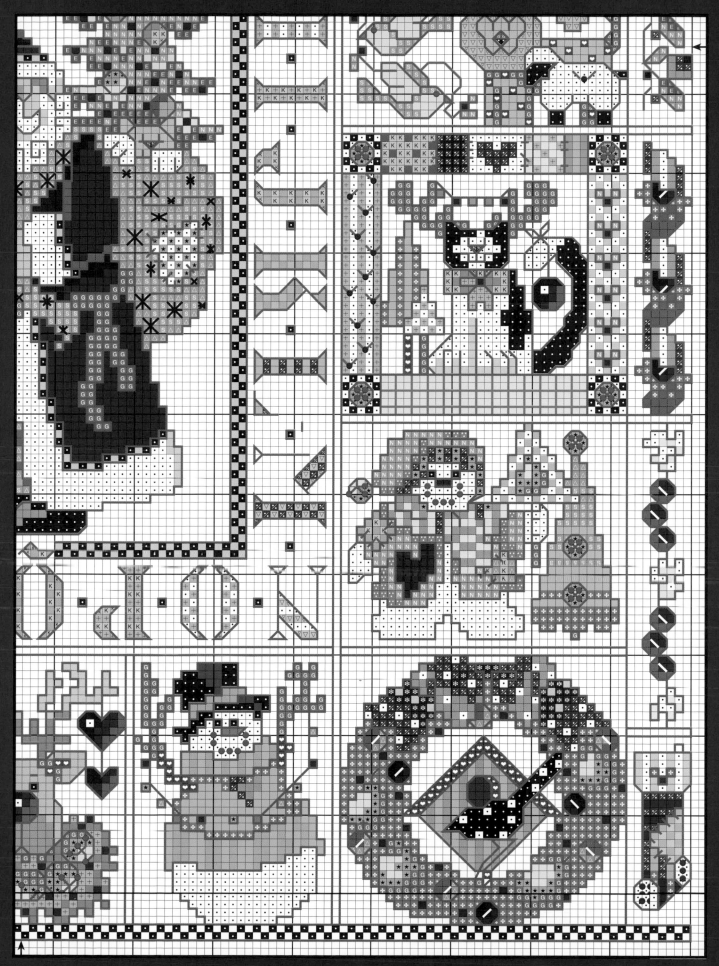

Folk Art Christmas Sampler

Stitched on: White Aida 14 over 1
Finished Design Size: 12" x 16"
Cut Fabric: 18" x 22"
Stitch Count: 168 x 224

Code for pages 10–13.

DMC Floss	XS	BS	FK	LS		DMC Floss	XS	BS	FK	LS
White	·			/		807	■			
745	□					806	H			/
676	▽					959	■			
3820	★					958	⠃			
945	■					3348	□			
742	−					989	N			
970	■			/		987	⠇			
608	■					986	E	⌐	●	
3716	■					702	■			
957	·					954	■			
956	⠿			/		911	✚			
666	■		●			699	■	⌐		
321	✳					3013	+			
815	■	⌐				3012	M			
210	■					3011	■			
553	■					3051	Z			/
550	■			/		928	■			
340	R					926	■			
3746	✦					3827	■			
775	□					976	G			
3325	■					301	♥			/
813	S					300	■			
826	△			/		3024	■			
311	■					647	■			
747	▨					3799	■	⌐	●	
598	K					310	■			

Stitch Count: 17 x 23

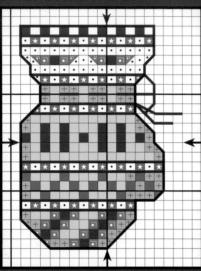

Stitch Count: 13 x 13

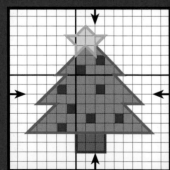

Stitch Count: 11 x 12

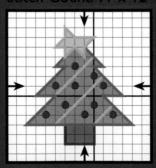

Stitch Count: 13 x 13

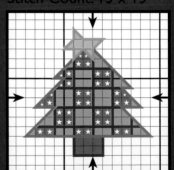

Stitch Count: 21 x 43

Stitch Count: 28 x 26

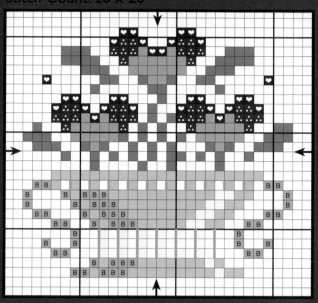

Code for pages 14–15.

Stitch Count: 50 x 30

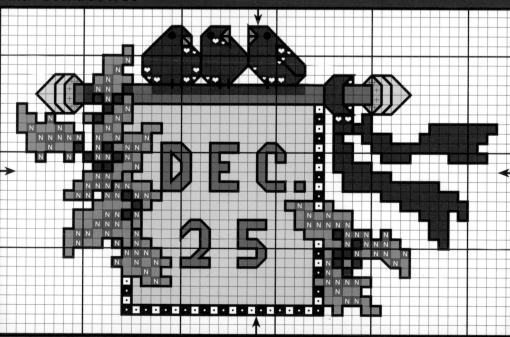

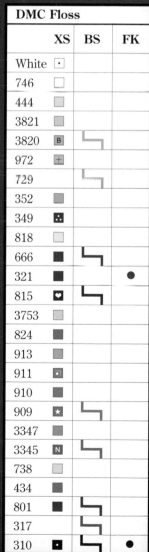

DMC Floss			
	XS	BS	FK
White	·		
746			
444			
3821			
3820	B		
972	+		
729			
352			
349			
818			
666			
321			●
815	♥		
3753			
824			
913			
911			
910			
909	★		
3347			
3345	N		
738			
434			
801			
317			
310			●

Stitch Count: 41 x 55

Stitch Count: 21 x 30

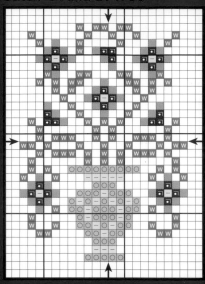

Stitch Count: 11 x 20

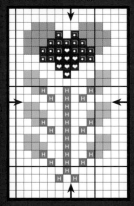

Stitch Count: 25 x 38

Stitch Count: 24 x 25

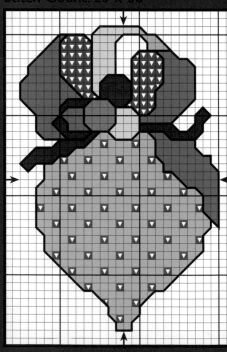

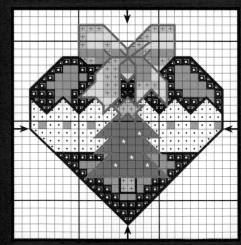

DMC Floss		
	XS	BS
White	·	
727	−	
444		
3821	◎	
972		
745		
676	+	
729		
352		
349	▣	
818		
321	■	
815	♥	⌐
3753		
798		
797	▽	
824	✳	
954		
911		
910	H	
909	★	⌐
700	W	
738		
434		⌐
801	■	⌐
317		⌐
310	▣	⌐

Stitch Count: 41 x 45

DMC Floss					DMC Floss			
	XS	BS	FK	LS		XS	BS	FK
White	·				797	▼		
745					796		⌐	
676	+				3817			
729	H			╲	3816	N		
444					924			
972	◎				913			
352					911			
350	■	⌐			909	★	⌐	
776	−	⌐			562	△		
666	◰	⌐			561	M		
321	■				907			
304		⌐	●		3347	✳		
815	E				738			
210					436			
3753					434		⌐	
3325					801		⌐	
793	⊡				310	■	⌐	●
798								

Stitch Count: 66 x 14

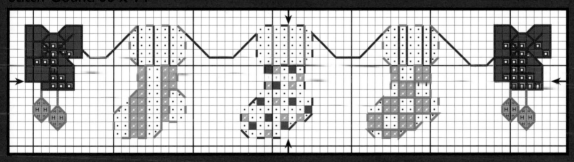

Stitch Count: 25 x 27

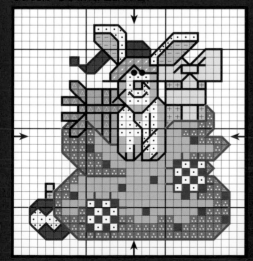

Stitch Count: 48 x 32

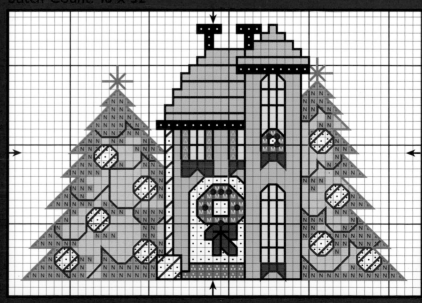

Stitch Count: 20 x 31

Stitch Count: 20 x 25

Stitch Count: 19 x 29

Stitch Count: 27 x 35

DMC Floss				DMC Floss				DMC Floss			
	XS	BS	FK		XS	BS	FK		XS	BS	FK
White	⊡			321	■			738	▨		
745	▧			815		⌐	●	436	▨		
676	+			3753	▨			434	■	⌐	
972	▨			3325	▨			801		⌐	
948	▨			798	▨			838	■		
818	−			796	▨	⌐		898		⌐	
776	▨			3816	◉			310	▣	⌐	●
3722	■			913	▨						
350	■			911	E						
666	★	⌐	●	909	▨	⌐	●				

Stitch Count: 45 x 40

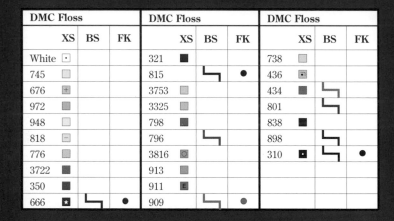

Stitch Count: 21 x 25

Stitch Count: 24 x 42

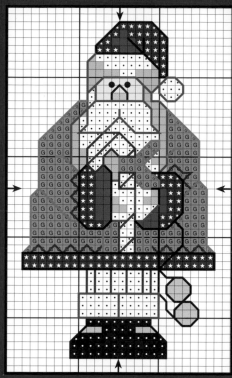

Stitch Count: 37 x 26

DMC Floss				DMC Floss				DMC Floss			
	XS				XS	BS	FK		XS	BS	FK
White	·			666	★	⌐	●	913	▨		
745	○			321	■			911	N		
744	+			304		⌐		909	B	⌐	
676	▨			815	♥			562	G		
729	◎			209	▨			561	■		
444	▨			3325	▨			738	▨		
972	△			799	E			436	H		
948	□			798	▣			434	▨		●
818	−			797	■			801	■		
776	▨			796		⌐		898		⌐	
351	S			824	▨			310	◨	⌐	●
350	■			772	▨						

Stitch Count: 42 x 34

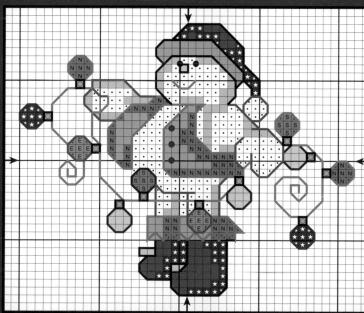

Stitch Count: 30 x 42

Stitch Count: 13 x 27

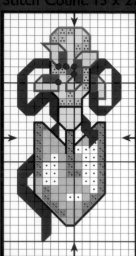

Stitch Count: 18 x 26

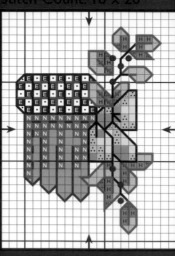

Stitch Count: 22 x 51

DMC Floss				DMC Floss			DMC Floss			
	XS	BS	FK		XS	BS		XS	BS	FK
White	·			3325	■		3816	H	⌐	
745	■			799	N		3818		⌐	
744	+			797	■	⌐	738	■		
972	■			796		⌐	436	△		
676	∴			824	★		434	■		
729	■			772	■		976		⌐	
948	■			913	◎		898		⌐	●
352	■			911	■		453	■		
666	■		●	909	◧	⌐	452	⊠		
321	E	⌐		562	▣		414	■		
815	■	⌐	●	3817	■		310	▣	⌐	●
209	■									

Stitch Count: 53 x 41

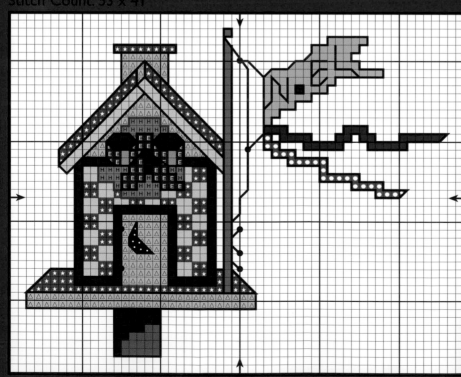

Stitch Count: 19 x 36

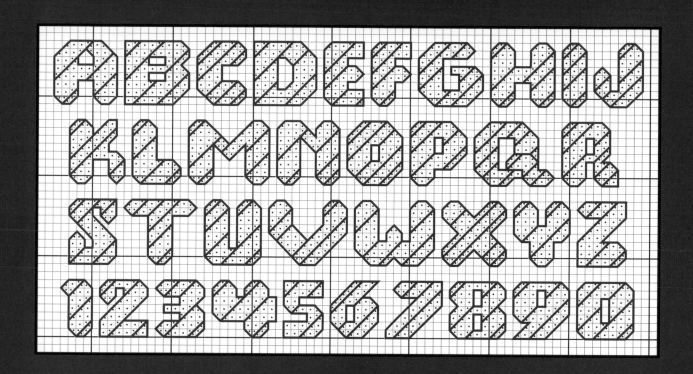

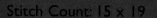
Stitch Count: 15 x 19

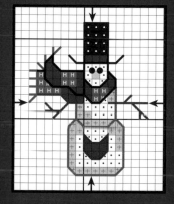

Stitch Count: 11 x 21

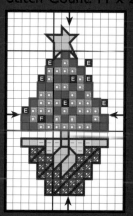

DMC Floss					DMC Floss			
	XS	HC	BS	FK		XS	BS	FK
White	·				796		⌐	
745					312		⌐	
744	−				913	⊡	⌐	
676					911	■		
776					909		⌐	
350	▨				3816	■		
666	■		⌐	●	3818		⌐	
321	E				561	H		
304			⌐		434		⌐	
554			╱		801		⌐	
800	⊞				310	⊡	⌐	●
3325								

Stitch Count: 76 x 32

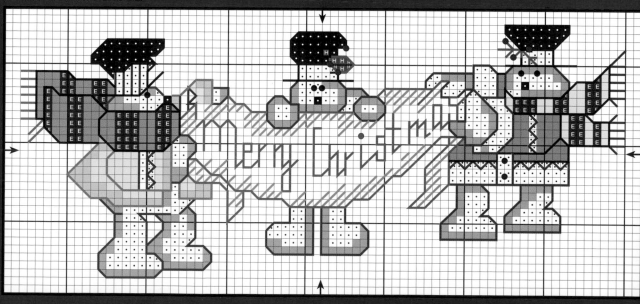

Stitch Count: 20 x 24

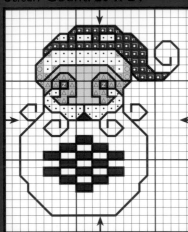

Stitch Count: 19 x 22

Stitch Count: 27 x 24

Stitch Count: 37 x 31

DMC Floss					DMC Floss			
	XS	BS	FK			XS	BS	FK
White	·				3345			
444					912			
972	+				911			
676					909		⌐	
729	B				3818			●
818					738			
666			●		436	△		
321			●		434			
815		⌐			801		⌐	
3753	○				453			
800					451			
798					415	S		
797	✳				413		⌐	●
824	Z	⌐			310	■	⌐	●
907								

Stitch Count: 26 x 35

Stitch Count: 32 x 38

Stitch Count: 37 x 35

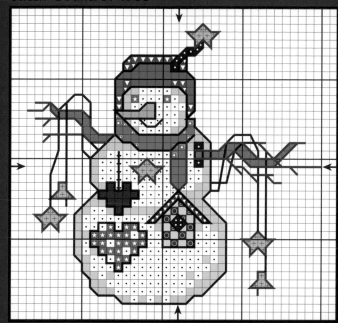

DMC Floss				DMC Floss			
	XS	BS	FK		XS	BS	FK
White	·			824	★		
444				907			
972	+			3347	E		
818				911			
352				909	⊡	⌐	
666	◎			738			
321	■	⌐	●	434			
815	♥			801	■	⌐	
3753				317			
798	■	⌐		310	⊡	⌐	●
797	▼						

Stitch Count: 35 x 14

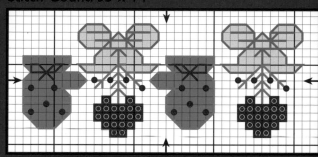

Stitch Count: 41 x 50

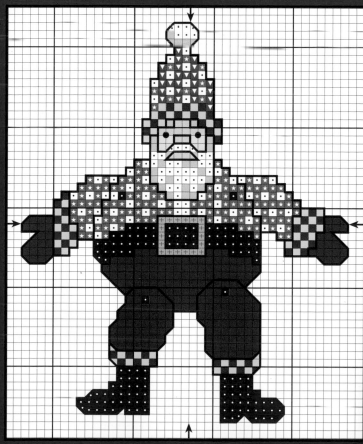

Stitch Count: 21 x 49

Santa
Christmas

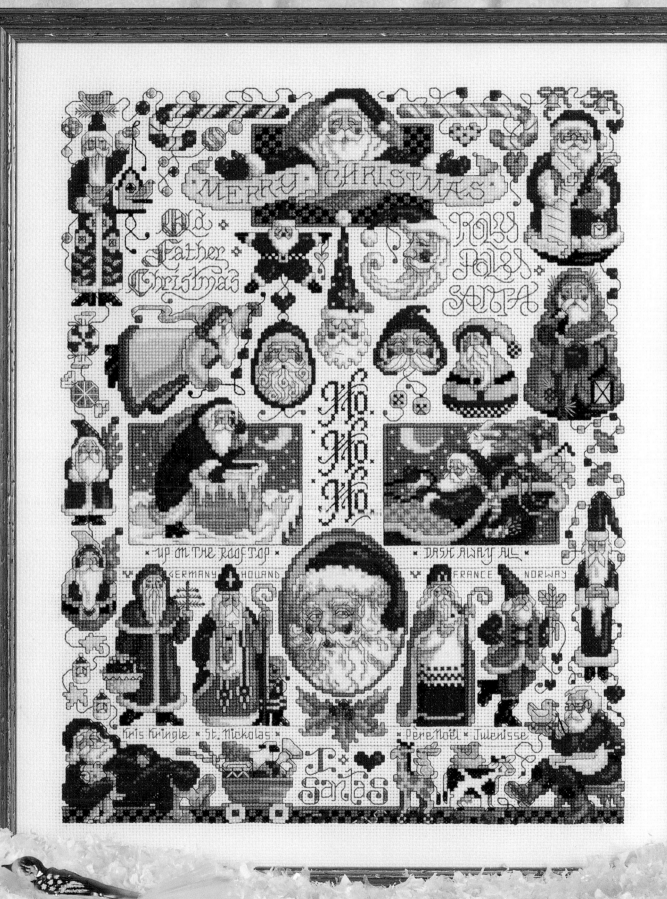

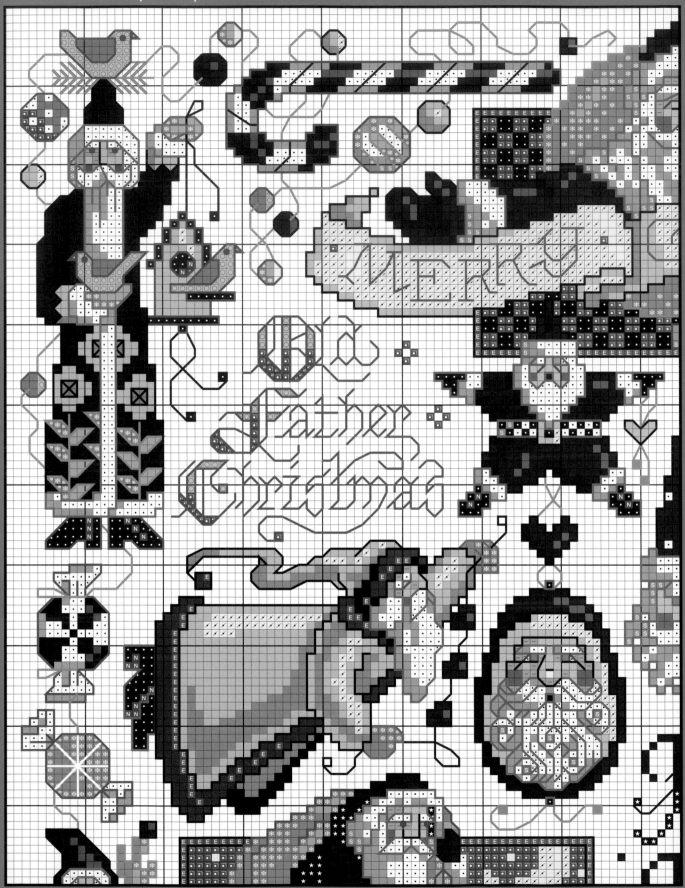

UP ON THE ROOFTOP

GERMANY • HOLLAND

Kris Kringle • St. Nickolas

DASH AWAY ALL

FRANCE   NORWAY

Père Noël · Julenisse

Santa Christmas Sampler

Stitched on: Antique White Aida 14 over 1
Finished Design Size: 12⅛" x 16"
Cut Fabric: 19" x 22"
Stitch Count: 169 x 224

Code for pages 26–29.

DMC Floss	XS	BS	FK	LS	DMC Floss	XS	BS	FK	LS
White	·			/	799	■			
3823	□				798	◙	⌐	●	
677	◹				703	■			
676	■				911 / 562	❋			/
729	■				991	■	⌐		
945	■				435	E			
758	⁻				433	■			
407	■				898 / 938	■			
3772	⣿				898		⌐		
351	■				3072 / 648	■			
666	■		●		647	S			
304	■			\	645	■	⌐		
902	★	⌐			844	N	⌐	●	\
828	□				310	⊡	⌐	●	\
519	◯	⌐							

Code for pages 30–31.

DMC Floss	XS	BS	FK	DMC Floss	XS	BS	FK
White	·			824	⣿		
Ecru	□			703	■		
744	■			702	★		
743	+			3347	■		
444	◯			890	■	⌐	
972	■		●	911	N		
783	◙			562	■		
780	■			561	⣿		
945	■			3818		⌐	
758	⁻			976		⌐	
818	■			738	□		
352	△			436	S		
351	■			3782	U		
349	■	⌐	●	3032	■		
666	✕			801	W	⌐	
321	H			898	■	⌐	
304	❋			648	■		
815	E			647	Z		
814	■			414	A		
3753	■			535	■	⌐	
813	■			310	⊡	⌐	●
798	■	⌐					

Stitch Count: 34 x 46

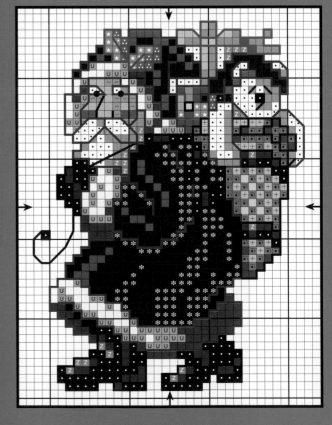

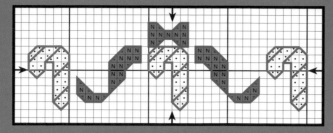

Stitch Count: 29 x 56

DMC Floss			DMC Floss				DMC Floss			
	XS	BS		XS	BS	FK		XS	BS	FK
White	·		815	♥		●	977	⊞		
Ecru			814	N			738			
744			3753				436	△		
743	−		3761	⊙			434			
783			813				3032	▣		
780	◈		798		⌐	●	801			
945			702	E		·	898		⌐	
758	◿		911				3782	✳		
351			909	★			648			
349		⌐	562	U			647	Z		
666	◩		561	W			535		⌐	
321	H		890		⌐		310	◪	⌐	●
304			3827	✕						

Stitch Count: 24 x 57

Stitch Count: 42 x 42

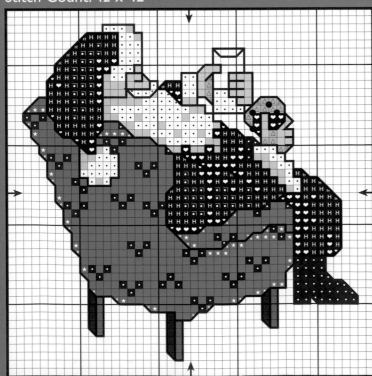

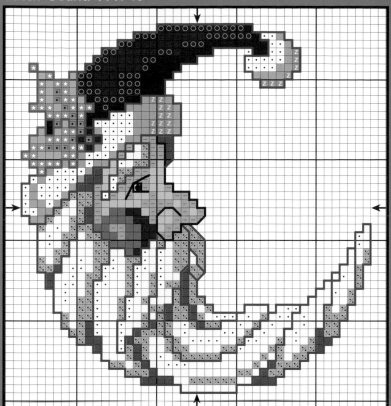

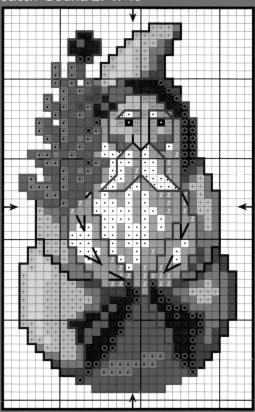

Stitch Count: 47 x 45

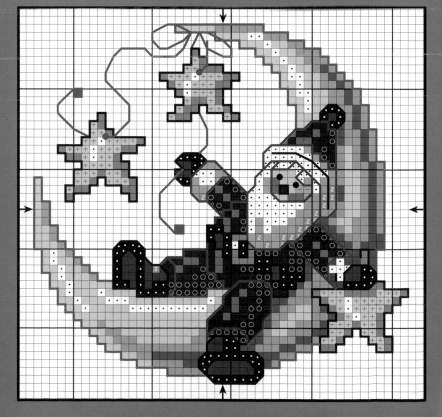

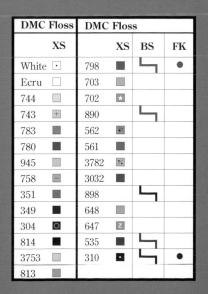

DMC Floss		DMC Floss			
	XS		**XS**	**BS**	**FK**
White	·	798	■	⌐	●
Ecru	☐	703	▣		
744	▣	702	★		
743	+	890	■	⌐	
783	▣	562	▣		
780	■	561	■		
945	▣	3782	▨		
758	▣	3032	■		
351	▣	898	■	⌐	
349	■	648	▣		
304	◉	647	Z		
814	■	535	■		
3753	▣	310	▪	⌐	●
813	■				

Stitch Count: 28 x 30

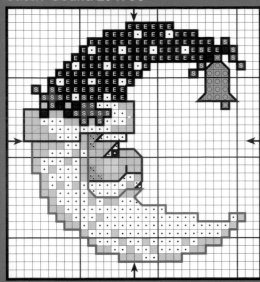

DMC Floss			DMC Floss				DMC Floss			
	XS	BS		XS	BS	FK		XS	BS	FK
White	·		321	E		●	890		⌐	
744			304				738			
743	+		815	♡	⌐		437	△		
972	◎		814	H	⌐		436	▨		
783		⌐	3753				435			
945			703				898		⌐	
758	–		702	★			648			
818			912				647	Z		
351			562	·			317		⌐	
349	⁙		561	✳	⌐		535		⌐	●
666			3345	S			310	⁙	⌐	●

Stitch Count: 28 x 56

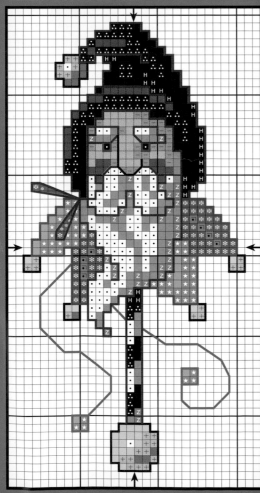

Stitch Count: 43 x 48

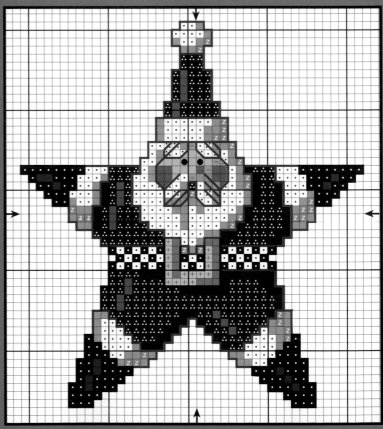

Stitch Count: 43 x 16

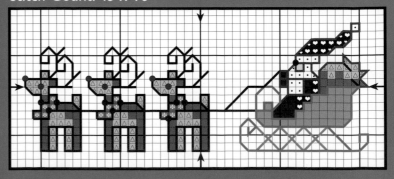

Stitch Count: 36 x 36

Stitch Count: 19 x 24

Stitch Count: 36 x 36

DMC Floss			
	XS	**BS**	**FK**
White	·		
744			
783	✕	⌐	●
951			
945	B		
760			
947			
349			
304	◎		
814		⌐	
3753			
932	▫		
931		⌐	
471	▨		
3347			
986		⌐	
840			
839			
898	A	⌐	
415			
414	Z	⌐	
310	▪		

Stitch Count: 43 x 115

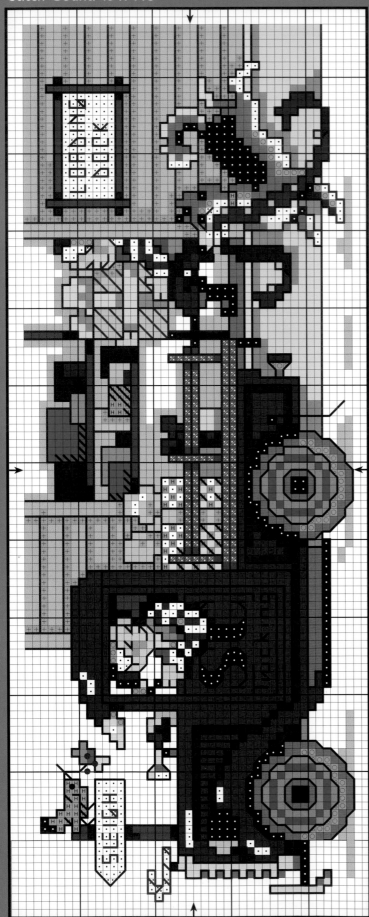

Stitch Count: 27 x 36

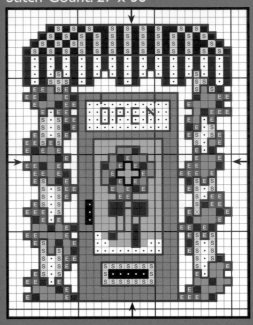

Stitch Count: 25 x 21

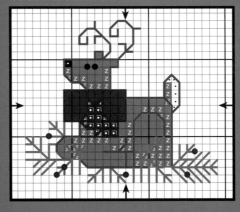

DMC Floss				DMC Floss			
	XS	BS	FK		XS	BS	FK
White	·			3827	▨		
725	▨			977	+		
951	▨			841	▨		
894	▨			435	▨		
666	■	⌐	●	434	z		
321	⊡		●	3826	▨		
304		⌐		400	■		
815	■	⌐		898	■	⌐	
3766	▨			762	▨		
996	H			3072	s		
3348	▨			415	◎		
3347	▨			318	▨		
702	▨			413		⌐	
986	■			535		⌐	
909	E	⌐		310	■	⌐	●
561		⌐					

Stitch Count: 51 x 109

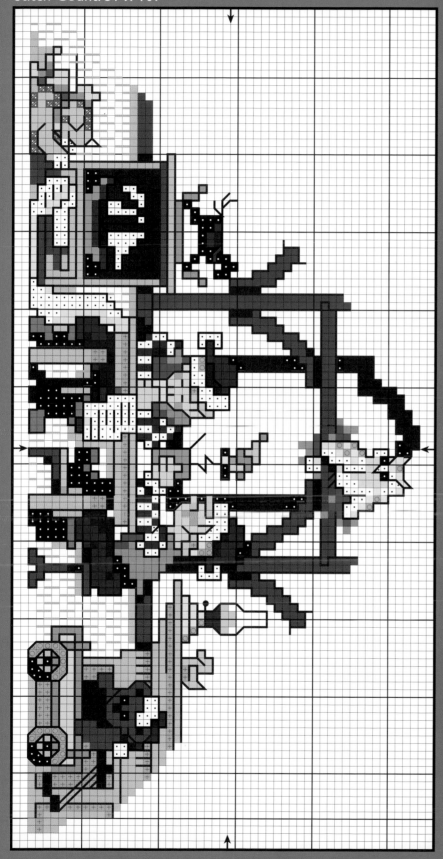

Stitch Count: 14 x 21

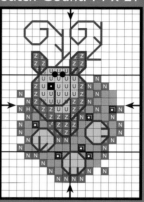

Stitch Count: 14 x 31

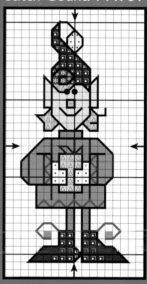

DMC Floss			DMC Floss			
	XS	BS		XS	BS	FK
White	·		912			
744	△		561	N		
725			3816			
676			3818		⌐	
951			3827			
948			977	+	⌐	
776	–		437	U		
894			434	Z		
350	✳		3826	⬚		
666	■	⌐	400	■		
321	▣		801		⌐	
304		⌐	898	■	⌐	●
815	■		762			
996			415	◉		
3348			318	■		
3347			413		⌐	
986	■		310	■	⌐	●

Stitch Count: 33 x 43

DMC Floss			DMC Floss			
	XS	BS		XS	BS	FK
White	·		561		⌐	
725			3827			
951			977	+	⌐	
894			3826			
666		⌐	400			
304		⌐	898		⌐	●
815			762			
996			415	○		
3348			318			
3347			310	·	⌐	
986						

Stitch Count: 44 x 9

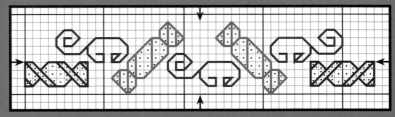

Stitch Count: 71 x 42

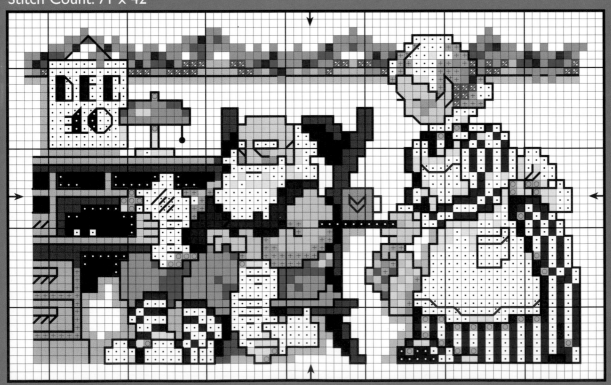

38

Stitch Count: 23 x 33

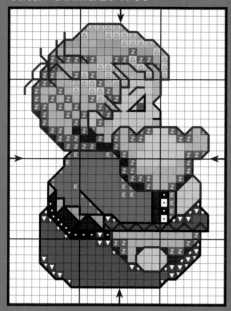

Stitch Count: 22 x 34

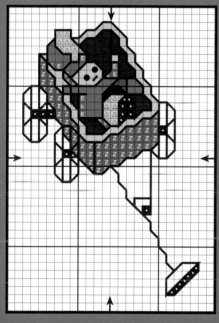

DMC Floss		DMC Floss		DMC Floss				
XS		**XS**			**XS**	**BS**	**FK**	**LS**
White	·	210		842				
3078		208		841				
444	△	3766		738				
972		798		436				
742	✳	797	▼	434	Z			
740		796	M	801				
945		702		3072	☒			
666		911		535				
815		909	E	310	■		●	/

Stitch Count: 46 x 36

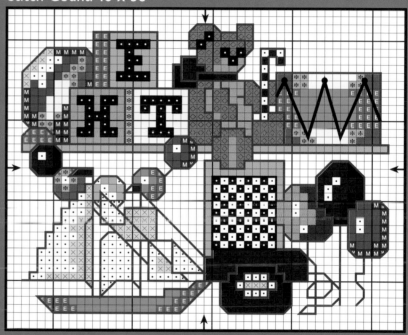

Stitch Count: 65 x 25

Stitch Count: 31 x 36

DMC Floss		
	XS	**BS**
White	·	
744		
783		
676	◎	
729		⌐
951		
945	B	
760		
349	◙	
304		
814		⌐
931		
471	⊡	
3347		
986		⌐
840		
898		⌐
415		
414	Z	⌐

Stitch Count: 34 x 34

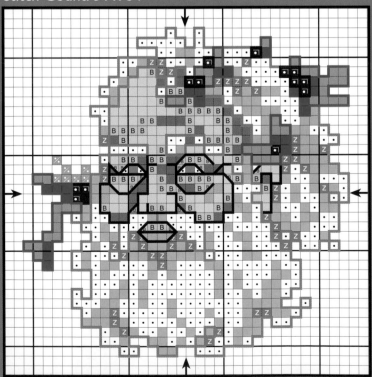

Stitch Count: 21 x 25

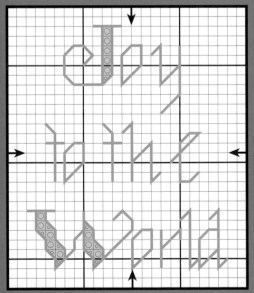

Stitch Count: 36 x 36

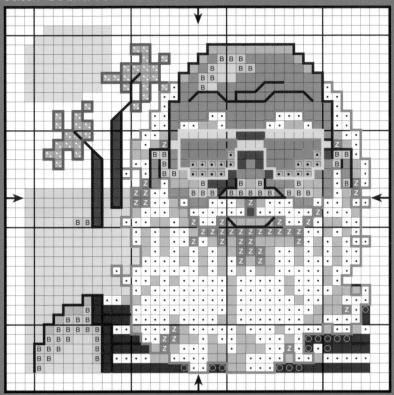

Stitch Count: 25 x 33

Stitch Count: 36 x 36

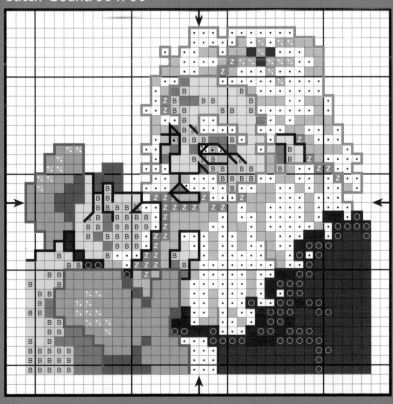

DMC Floss			
	XS	BS	FK
White	·		
744			
783			
951			
945	B		
760			
349			
666			
321	+		
304	○		
814			
3753			
932	·		
931			
813			
312			
471			
3347			
701			
700			
986			●
840			
839			
898			
415			
414	Z		

Stitch Count: 36 x 36

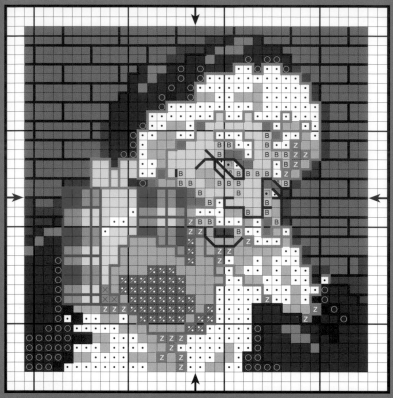

Stitch Count: 18 x 27

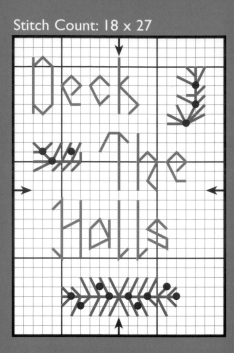

Stitch Count: 36 x 36

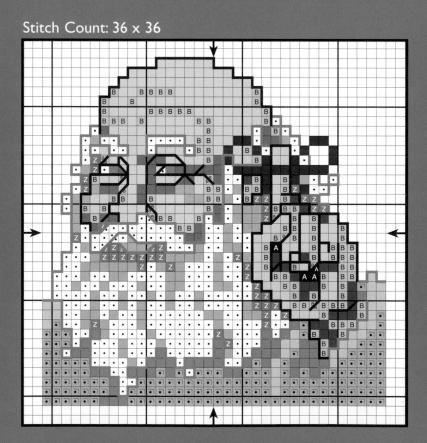

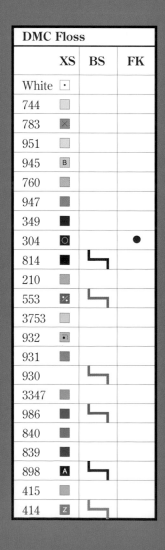

DMC Floss				
		XS	**BS**	**FK**
White	·			
744				
783	✕			
951				
945	B			
760				
947				
349				
304	◎			●
814			⌐	
210				
553	⅍		⌐	
3753				
932	·ı			
931				
930			⌐	
3347				
986			⌐	
840				
839				
898	A		⌐	
415				
414	Z		⌐	

Stitch Count: 34 x 17

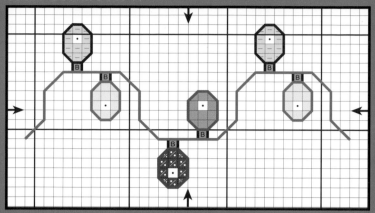

Stitch Count: 36 x 18

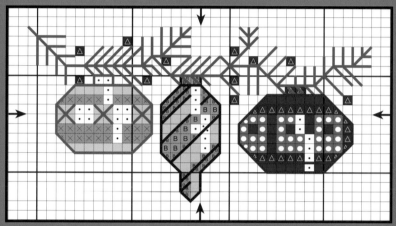

Stitch Count: 36 x 18

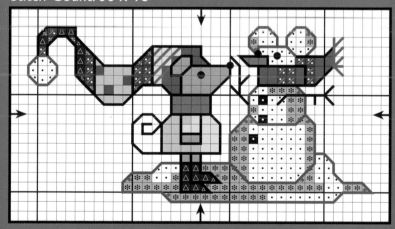

Stitch Count: 36 x 13

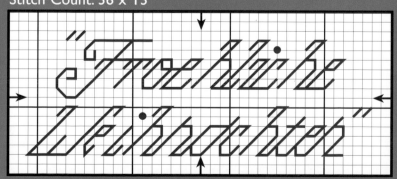

Stitch Count: 32 x 8

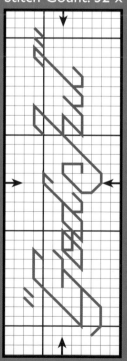

DMC Floss			
	XS	**BS**	**FK**
White	·		
745			
744	—		
676			
729	B		
351			
350			
666	■	⌐	●
321	△		
304		⌐	
800			
3325	✳		
813			
826	✕		
798			
312		⌐	
772			
909	⬚		
561	■	⌐	
3818		⌐	
898		⌐	
452			
310	■	⌐	●

Stitch Count: 39 x 10

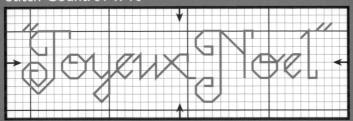

Stitch Count: 14 x 73

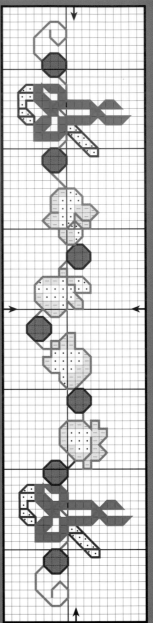

Stitch Count: 35 x 20

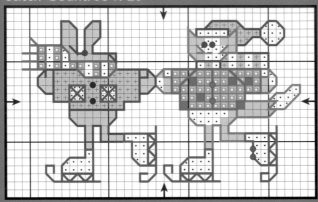

Stitch Count: 32 x 26

DMC Floss			DMC Floss				DMC Floss			
	XS	BS		XS	BS	FK		XS	BS	FK
White	·		321	☒		●	561		⌐	
745	–		304		⌐		437	▣		
744	▢		3722	■			434		⌐	
676	◎		800	▢			801		⌐	
976		⌐	312		⌐	●	413		⌐	●
948	▢		913	▣			310		⌐	●
776	+		911	■						
666	■	⌐								

Stitch Count: 26 x 35

Stitch Count: 25 x 33

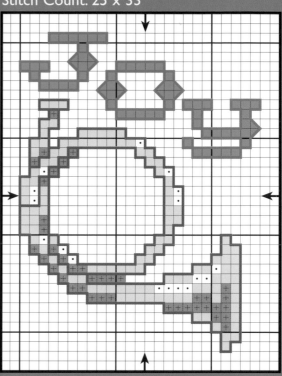

Stitch Count: 36 x 36

DMC Floss			
	XS	**BS**	**FK**
White	·		
744			
783	+		
780		⌐	
951			
945	B		
947			
760			
349			
304			
814	◨	⌐	
932			
931		⌐	
471			
3347	✳		
986		⌐	
701			
700		⌐	
420			
840			
898	A	⌐	
415			
414	Z	⌐	
310	◼	⌐	●

Stitch Count: 34 x 36

DMC Floss			
	XS	**BS**	**FK**
White	·		
744			
783			
780			●
951			
945	B		
760			
349			
304			
814	⊡		
931			
930			●
471	%		
3347			
986			
840			
839			
898	A		
415			
414	Z		

Stitch Count: 21 x 36

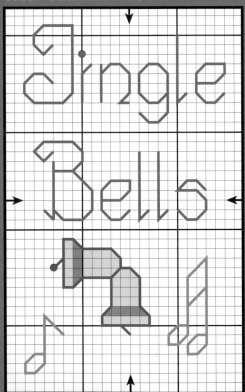

Stitch Count: 32 x 36

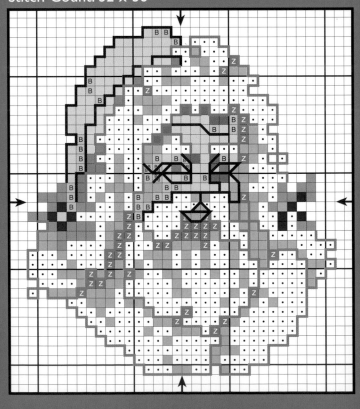

Stitch Count: 36 x 36

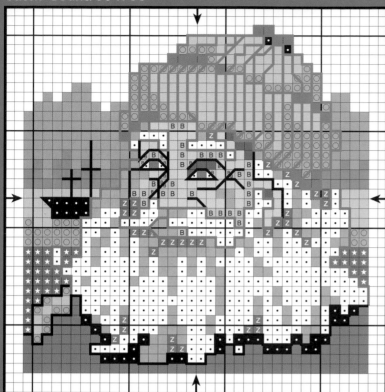

Stitch Count: 23 x 24

Stitch Count: 30 x 36

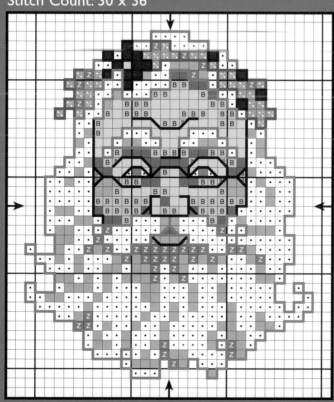

DMC Floss		
	XS	**BS**
White	·	
744		
783		
780		⌐
951		
945	B	
760		
349		
666	+	
304		
814		⌐
210		
3753		
932	○	
931		⌐
471	%	
3347		
986		⌐
420	★	
840		
898		⌐
415		
414	Z	⌐
310	▪	⌐

Stitch Count: 36 x 36

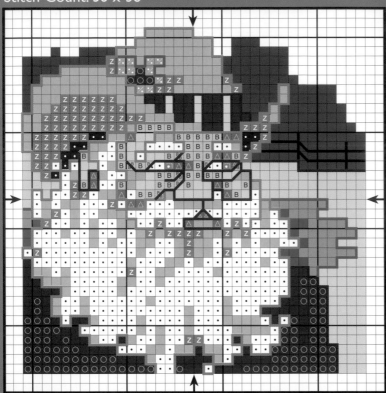

DMC Floss		
	XS	**BS**
White	·	
744		
951		
945	B	
760		
666		⌐
349	○	
304		
814		⌐
932		
931	◌	
930		⌐
471	⦂	
3347		
986		⌐
420	★	
842		
840	△	
839		⌐
898	A	⌐
415		
414	Z	⌐
310	■	⌐

Stitch Count: 21 x 28

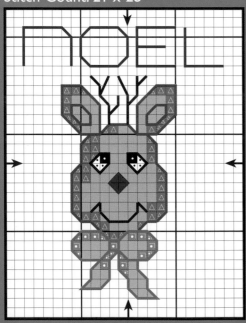

Stitch Count: 36 x 36

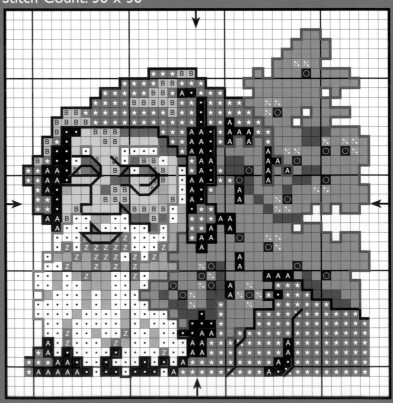

Stitch Count: 23 x 32

Stitch Count: 26 x 34

Stitch Count: 35 x 35

DMC Floss			
	XS	**BS**	**FK**
White	·		
744			
783	+	⌐	
729			
780		⌐	
951			
945	B		
760			
666		⌐	
349	◉		
304			
814	✦	⌐	
3753			
932	▣		
931			
813	✕		
312		⌐	
471	▨		
3347			
701	△		
700		⌐	
840			
839	H		
898		⌐	
415			
414	Z		
310	■	⌐	●

Stitch Count: 36 x 36

Stitch Count: 21 x 23

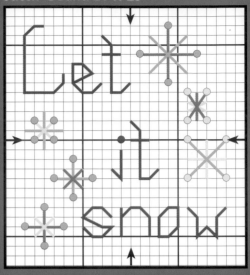

Stitch Count: 36 x 36

DMC Floss			
	XS	**BS**	**FK**
White	·		
744		⌐	
783			
947	+		
951			
945	B		
760			
349	○		
304			
814	N	⌐	
3756		⌐	●
3325		⌐	●
334		⌐	
312		⌐	●
3753			
932	·		
931		⌐	
471	⊠		
3347			
986		⌐	
840			
839	E		
898		⌐	
415			
414	Z	⌐	
310	·	⌐	

Stitch Count: 32 x 34

Stitch Count: 23 x 24

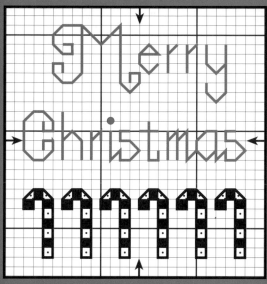

Stitch Count: 36 x 36

DMC Floss			
	XS	**BS**	**FK**
White	·		
744			
783			
947	╫		
951			
945	B		
760			
666		⌐	
349	◎		
304			
814	N	⌐	
210			
553	△		
931		⌐	
471			
3347			
700		⌐	●
986		⌐	
840			
839	E		
898		⌐	
415			
414	Z	⌐	
310	·	⌐	

Stitch Count: 36 x 36

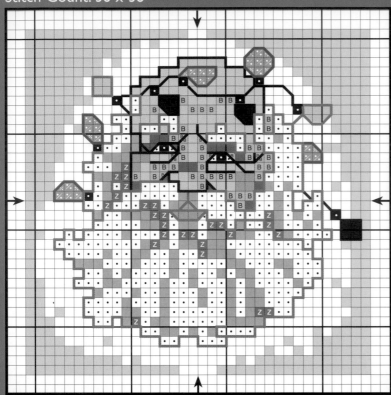

Stitch Count: 19 x 21

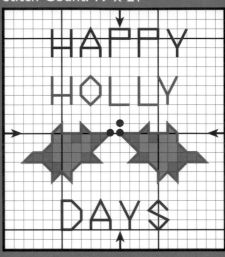

Stitch Count: 36 x 35

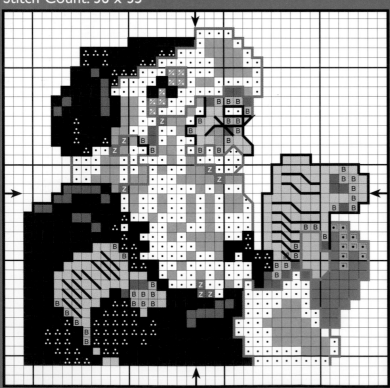

DMC Floss			
	XS	BS	FK
White	·		
744			
951			
945	B		
947			
760			
666		⌐	●
349			
304	⊡		
814		⌐	
3753			
932	⊡		
931		⌐	
471	⊡		
701			
700			
699		⌐	
986		⌐	
840			
898		⌐	
415			
414	Z	⌐	
310	⊡	⌐	

Stitch Count: 37 x 37

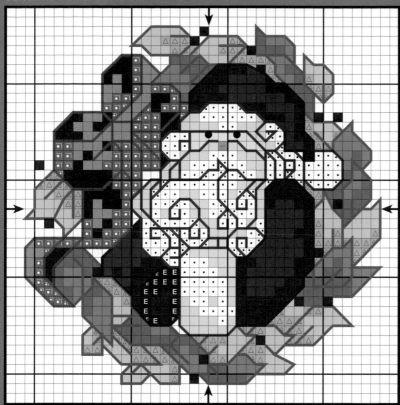

Stitch Count: 15 x 28

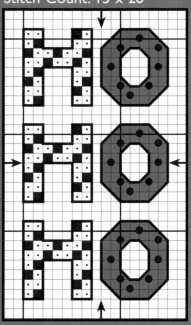

Stitch Count: 31 x 35

DMC Floss			
	XS	BS	FK
White	·		
744			
948			
947			
3716			
350			
349	◉		
666	■		●
304	▦		
816		⌐	
815	E		
814	■	⌐	
341			
340	▪		
333	■		
775			
798		⌐	
796		⌐	
3347			
564			
563	△		
701			
700			
699		⌐	
415			
414		⌐	
310	▪	⌐	●

Stitch Count: 43 x 24

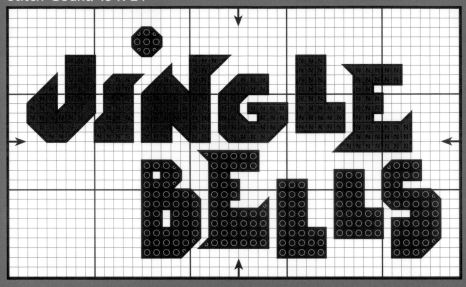

Stitch Count: 17 x 24

Code for pages 54–55.

DMC Floss			DMC Floss				DMC Floss			
	XS	FK		XS	BS	FK		XS	BS	FK
White	·		304	■	⌐		909	◱		
746	☐		800	☐			561	H		
744	☐		813	✕			3816	☐		
948	☐		798	■	⌐		3818		⌐	
776	–	●	312	■	⌐	●	738	☐		
351	■		703	☐			3827	⊡		
350	N		702	★			801		⌐	
349	■		890	■	⌐		413		⌐	●
666	◪		912	■			310	■	⌐	●
321	◙	●	911	✳		●				

Stitch Count: 25 x 22

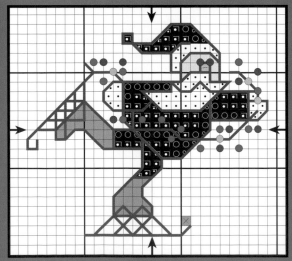

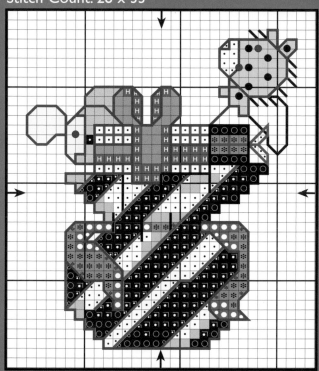

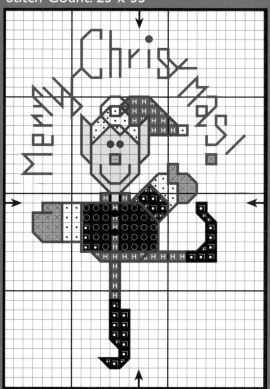

Stitch Count: 42 x 42

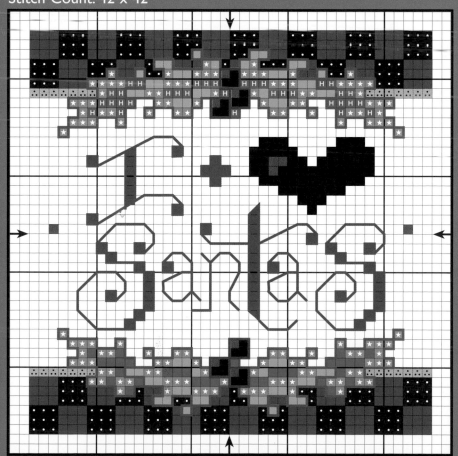

Inspirational
Christmas

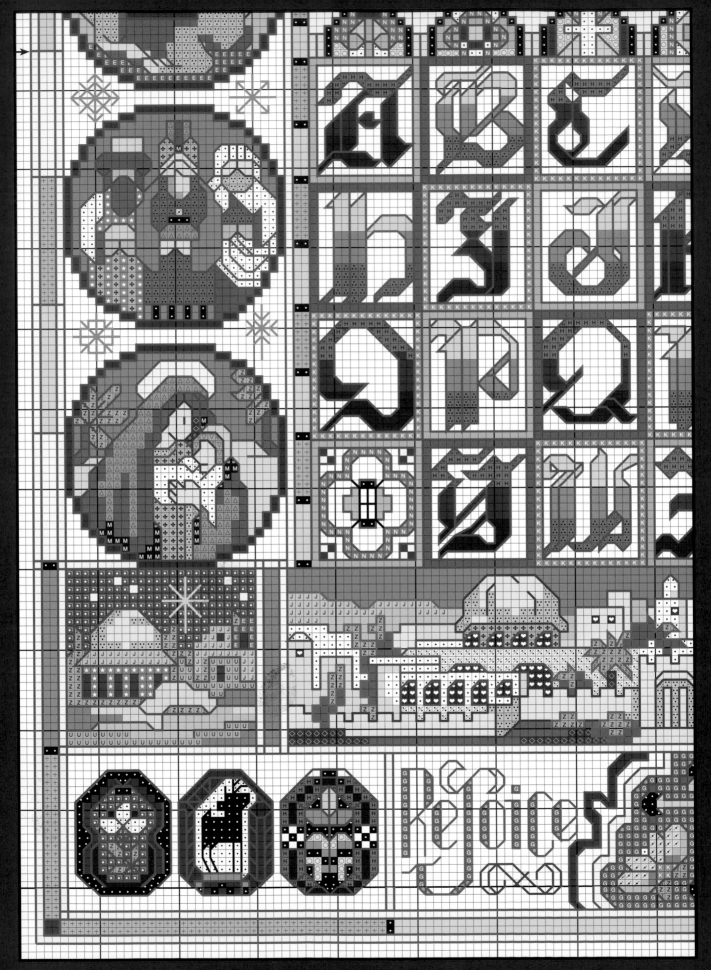

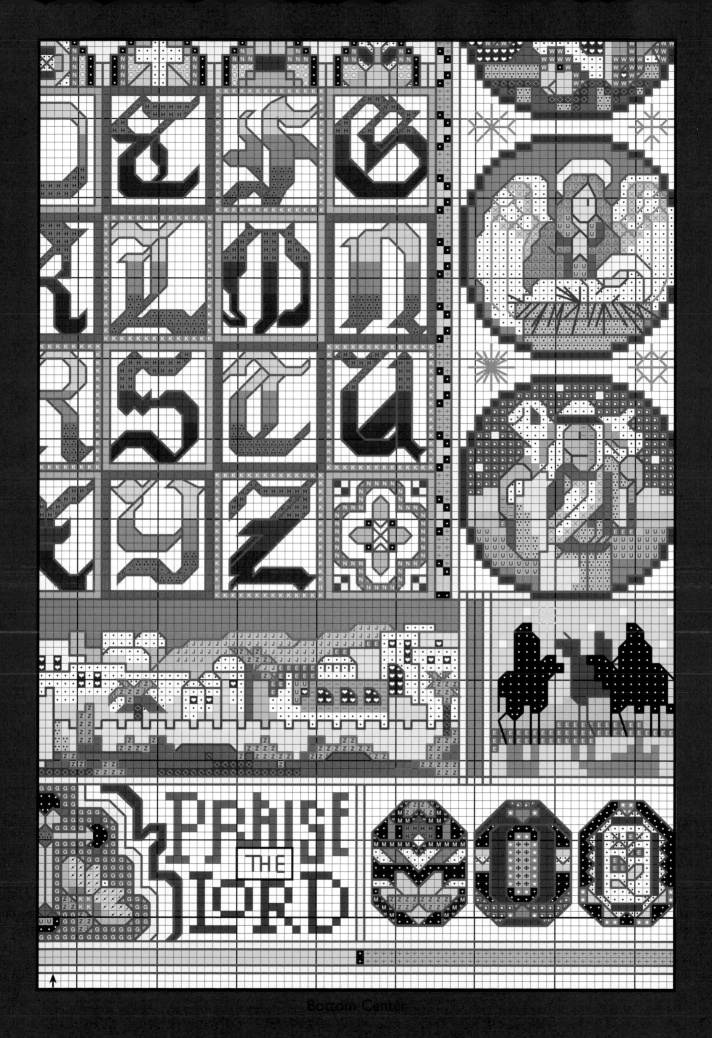

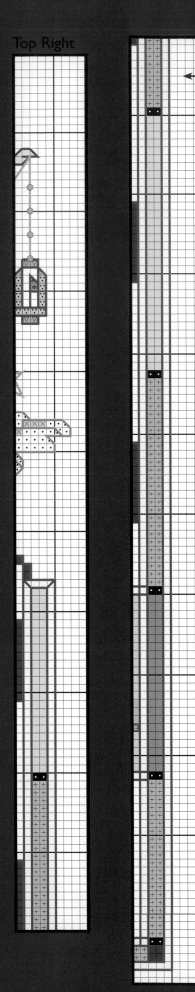

Bottom Right

Inspirational Christmas Sampler

Stitched on: Antique White Aida 14 over 1
Finished Design Size: 12¼" × 16¼"
Cut Fabric: 19" × 23"
Stitch Count: 170 × 225

Code for pages 58–62.

DMC Floss	XS	BS	FK	LS	DMC Floss	XS	BS	FK	LS
White	·				3766	▪			
3078	▫				3760	N			
744	▪	⌐		╲	772	○			
742	+				704	▪			
741	▪				702	▪			
948	▫				369	▪			
754	▪				954	Z			
758	−				912	K	⌐		
970	H				561	▪	⌐		
946	⁂				964	J			
606	▪	⌐	●	╲	959	+			
818	⁄				958	★	⌐		
776	▪				3045		⌐		
899	▪				3045 / 002	>▪	⌐		╲
335	S	⌐		╲	739	▫			
321	▪	⌐			437	⁑			
3609	▪				435	▪			
3608	▪				433	◇			
718	▪				402	▪			
211	▪				922	▪			
209	▪				920	▪			
208	▪	⌐			400	▪	⌐		
3747	▫				762	▫			
340	▪				415	▪			
775	▫				318	W			
3325	▪				317	▪			
799	▪	⌐		╲	413	♥			
798	▪	⌐			3799		⌐	●	
797	▪	⌐			310	▪	⌐		
747	⁒								

Stitch Count: 23 x 18

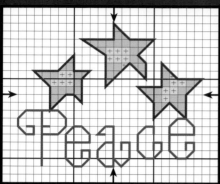

Stitch Count: 38 x 22

Stitch Count: 18 x 25

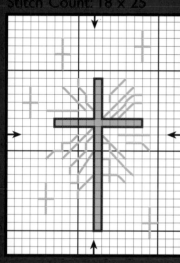

Stitch Count: 16 x 30

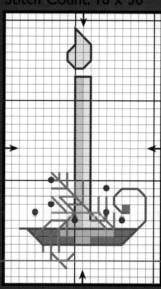

Stitch Count: 32 x 32

Stitch Count: 32 x 36

DMC Floss				DMC Floss		
	XS	**BS**	**FK**		**XS**	**BS**
White	⊡			3325		
745				798		
744	+			797	▼	
444	◎			312		⌐
676				909		⌐
972		⌐		907		
818				3347	E	
352				3345		
666	⊡		●	738		
321				436	—	
304		⌐		434		⌐
209		⌐		801		⌐
552				317		⌐
3753				310	⊡	⌐

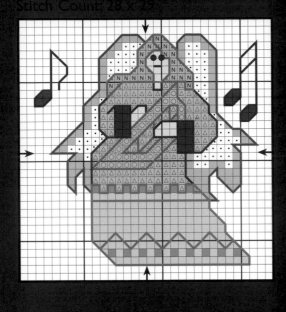

Stitch Count: 28 x 29

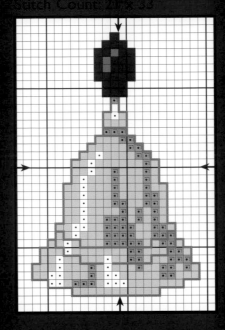

Stitch Count: 21 x 33

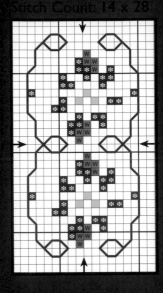

Stitch Count: 14 x 28

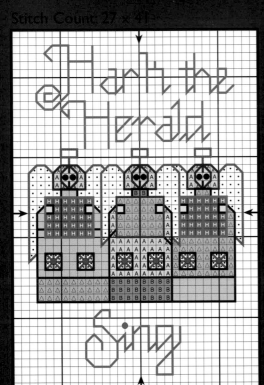

Stitch Count: 27 x 41

Stitch Count: 29 x 17

Stitch Count: 39 x 36

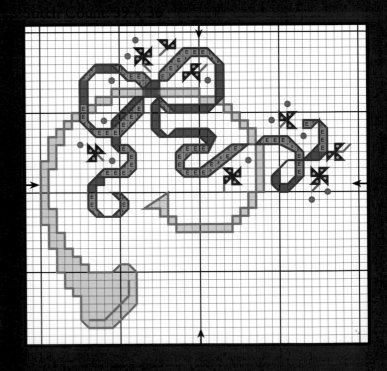

DMC Floss				DMC Floss				DMC Floss			
	XS				XS	BS	FK		XS	BS	FK
White	·			350	■			700			●
745	A			666	✳	⌐		3346	W		●
3822				304		⌐		562			
725				498	■			561	H	⌐	
676	◎			3325				3829			
729	B			809	E			436	N		
3820	·|			798		⌐	●	434		⌐	
948				796		⌐		801		⌐	●
947				312		⌐	●	413		⌐	
776	△			3817				310		⌐	●

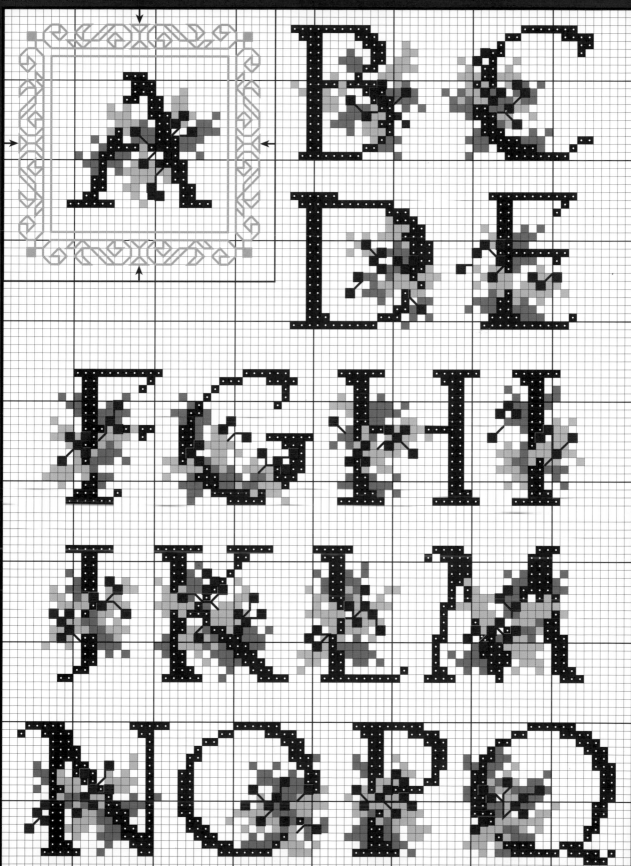

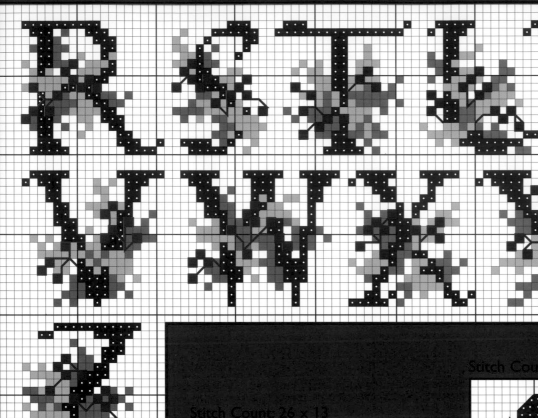

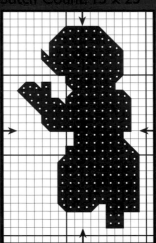

Stitch Count: 26 x 13

Stitch Count: 15 x 25

Code for pages 65–67.

DMC Floss		
	XS	**BS**
3820		
349		
704		
700		
310		

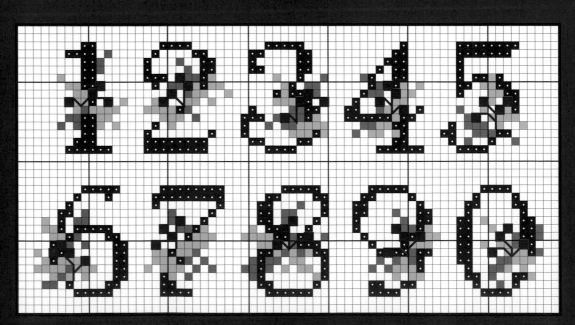

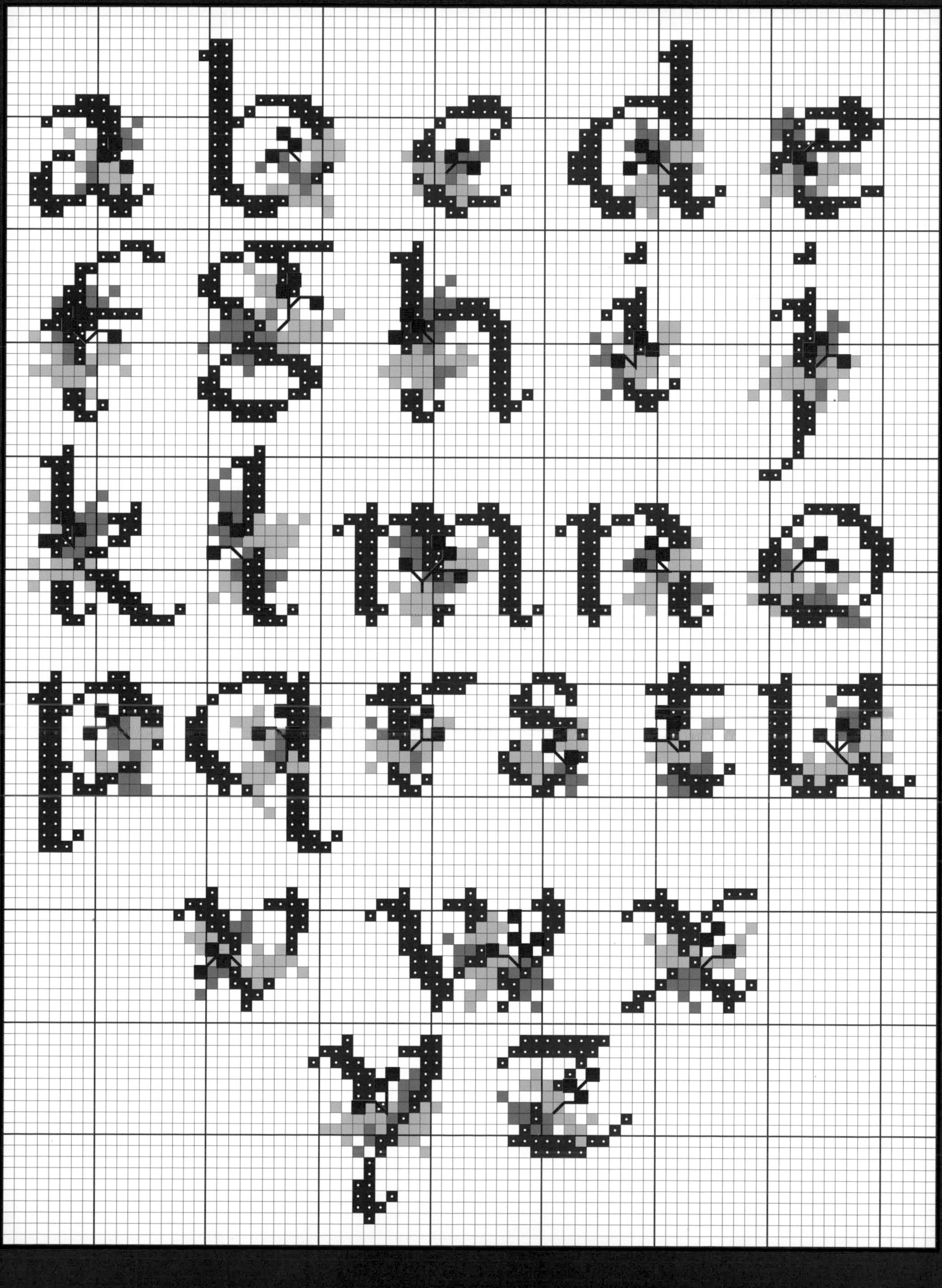

Stitch Count: 27 x 35

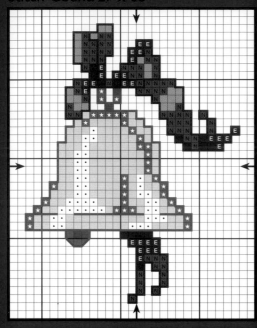

Stitch Count: 28 x 24

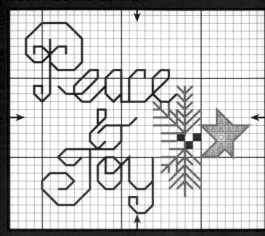

Stitch Count: 24 x 19

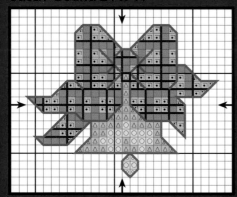

DMC Floss			DMC Floss			DMC Floss		
	XS	BS		XS	BS		XS	BS
White	·		666	■		3051	■	⌐
746	□		817	E		909		
745	○		815	■	⌐	700	■	
3823	−		3747	■		699		⌐
3822	■		340	Z		738	■	
727	+		3756	✖		436	H	
725	■		775	S		434		⌐
676	△		3755	■		3829	■	⌐
729	■		322	■		762	■	
3820	✳	⌐	3817	▪		318	★	
921		⌐	3816	■		317	■	⌐
352	■		522	■		310		⌐
350	N							

Stitch Count: 23 x 37

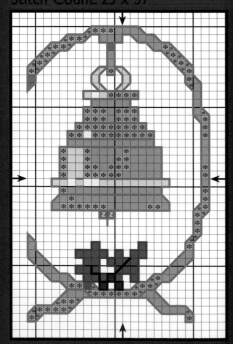

Stitch Count: 27 x 40

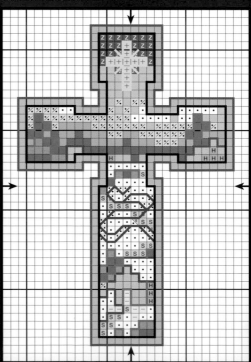

68

Stitch Count: 34 x 40

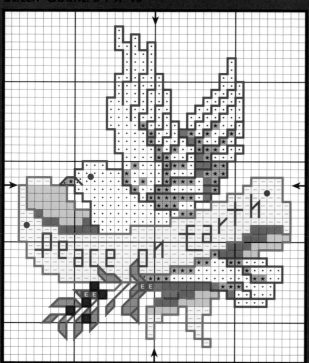

DMC Floss	XS	BS	FK	DMC Floss	XS	BS	DMC Floss	XS	BS	FK
White	·			776			436			
712				666	■	⌐	435	■		
822	−			816		⌐	422	H		
3822	⊠			369			3772	N	⌐	
3820		⌐		368	A		632	■	⌐	
676	△		●	367	■	⌐	840		⌐	
783	■			772	+		3828			
780		⌐		3347			762			
3770				3345	E	⌐	415	★		
945	◪			701			414	■		
758				699	▣		413		⌐	●
3778	◉			739	◇		310	▣	⌐	●
3064	■	⌐		437						

Stitch Count: 41 x 24

Stitch Count: 23 x 26

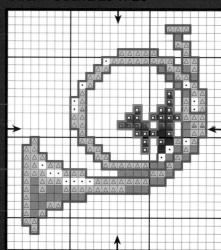

Stitch Count: 61 x 29

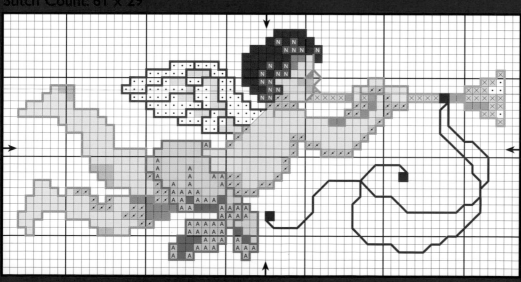

Stitch Count: 49 x 28

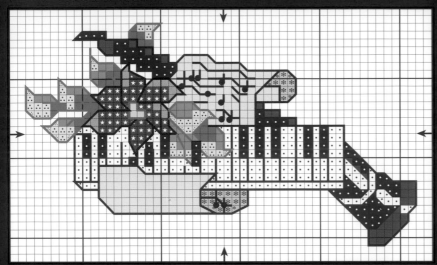

Stitch Count: 17 x 22

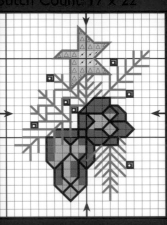

Stitch Count: 36 x 14

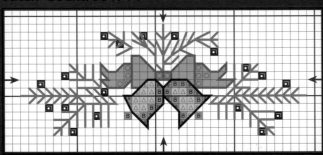

Stitch Count: 38 x 24

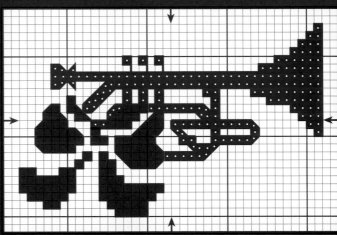

Stitch Count: 49 x 42

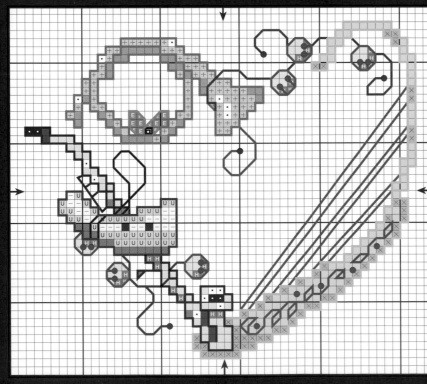

DMC Floss			DMC Floss				
	XS	BS		XS	BS	FK	LS
White	·		503	✕	⌐		
Ecru	−		702				
712			701	E	⌐		
745	◢		700		⌐		
727			356	★			
676	△		543	U			
729	B		738	✳			
3822	+		436				
3820			435				
353			434		⌐		
349	▣	⌐	3829		⌐		
666	■	⌐	841				
817		⌐	839	■	⌐	●	
826	◉		898		⌐		
813			762				
312		⌐	318	H			
772	⋰		413	■	⌐	●	╲
504			310	■	⌐	●	

Stitch Count: 20 x 29

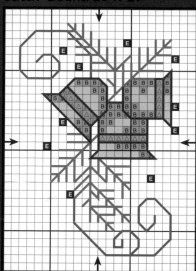

Stitch Count: 47 x 31

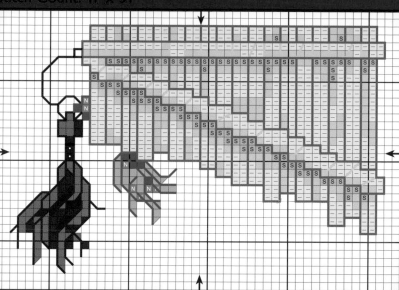

Stitch Count: 44 x 9

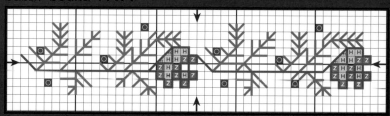

Stitch Count: 42 x 42

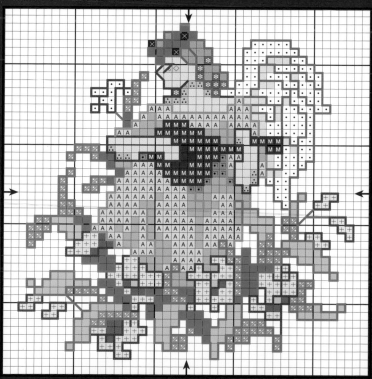

DMC Floss	XS	BS	DMC Floss	XS	BS
White	⋅		912		
712	–		910	■	⌐
3821	S		561		⌐
676			704		
729	B		701	N	⌐
3770			895		⌐
945			842		
963	◇		840	✳	⌐
351	■		869		⌐
350	○		739	+	
349	■		738		
666	✕		437	H	
321	E		435		
816	■	⌐	434	Z	
775	A		433	M	⌐
3325			801		⌐
518	▪	⌐	762		
813	△		317		⌐
312		⌐	413		⌐
939	■	⌐	310	▪	⌐
955					

Stitch Count: 31 x 39

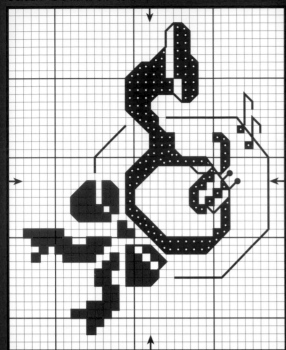

Stitch Count: 37 x 33

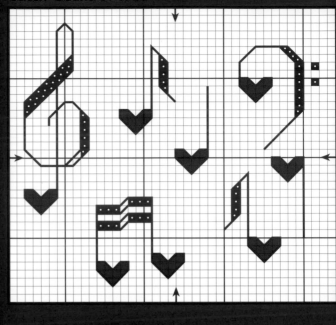

Stitch Count: 13 x 41

Stitch Count: 44 x 59

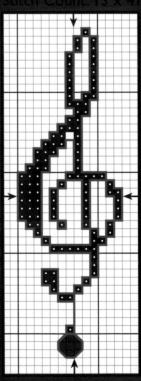

DMC Floss			DMC Floss			
	XS	BS		XS	BS	FK
746			911	■		
3822	+		3818		⌐	
3820	■		407	■		
3829		⌐	632	■		
666	■		413		⌐	
304	■		310	■	⌐	●
815		⌐				

72

Stitch Count: 30 x 38

Stitch Count: 25 x 51

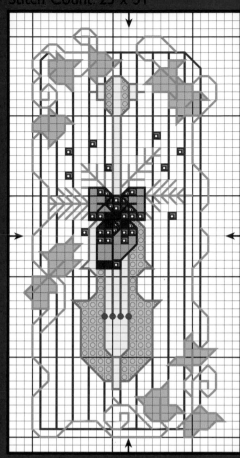

Stitch Count: 28 x 49

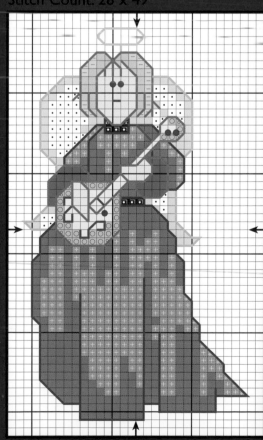

DMC Floss			DMC Floss		
	XS	**BS**		**XS**	**BS**	**FK**
White	·		333	■	⌐	
744	–		775	▢		
743	▫		3325		⌐	
677	▫		794	+		
676	⊙	⌐	793	■		
948	▫		796		⌐	
3326	▣		564	F		
350	E		563	▣		
666	■		562		⌐	
321	▣	⌐	700	■		
815	■	⌐	434		⌐	
3747	▢		433		⌐	●

Stitch Count: 17 x 13

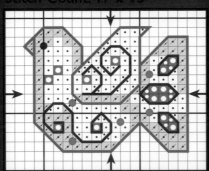

Stitch Count: 24 x 23

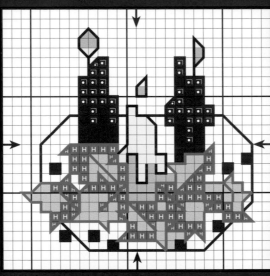

Stitch Count: 21 x 27

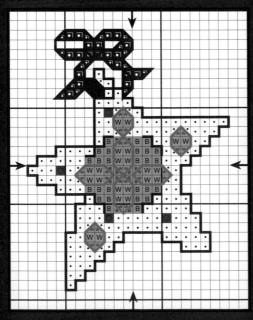

Code for pages 74–75.

DMC Floss	XS	BS	FK
White	·		
746			
3822			
676			
729	B		
781			
780			
758			
352	−		
351			
350			
349			
666			
304			
817			
775			
312			
954			
910			●
909			
772			
703	E		
3817			
3816	W		
561	H		
3772	N		
739	⊠		
435			
433	★		
898			
762			
318			
310			●

Stitch Count: 38 x 29

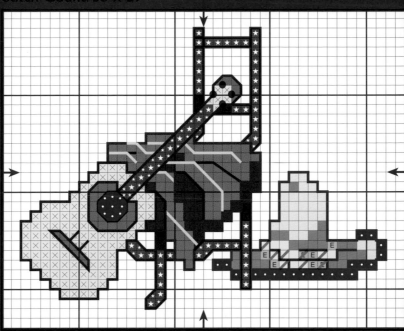

Stitch Count: 56 x 43

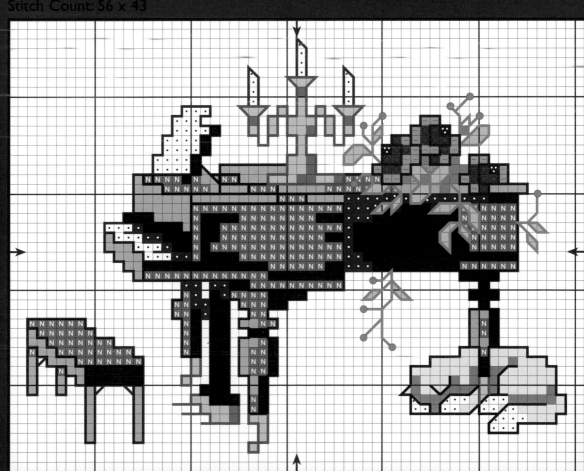

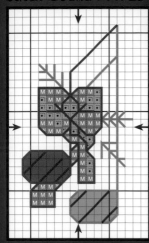

Stitch Count: 14 x 25

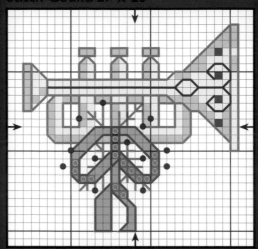

Stitch Count: 27 x 26

Stitch Count: 32 x 30

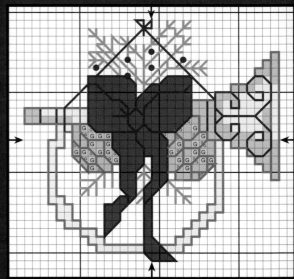

DMC Floss				DMC Floss		
	XS	BS	FK		XS	BS
677				794		
676				793		
350				796		
666				562		
321			●	702		
3747				700		
341				437	G	
340	M			436		
333				434		

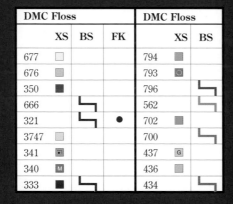

Stitch Count: 45 x 24

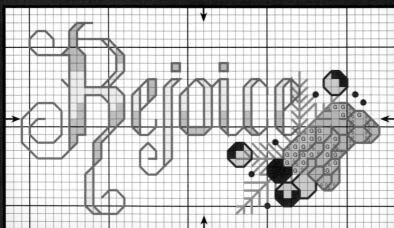

Stitch Count: 42 x 26

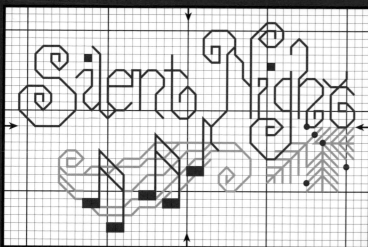

Stitch Count: 30 x 54

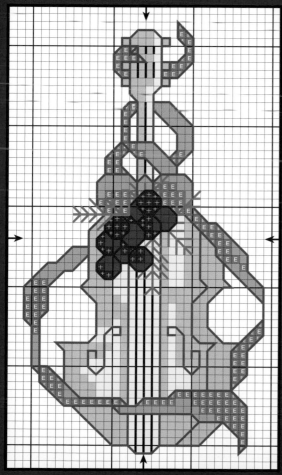

Stitch Count: 20 x 25

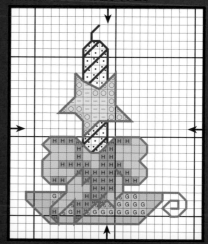

DMC Floss			
	XS	**BS**	**FK**
White	·		
745	–		
744	◎		
677	☐		
676	▨		
350	■	⌐	
666	+		
321	■	⌐	●
816		⌐	
333	■	⌐	
794	▨		
793	E		
796		⌐	
955	▨		
913	H		
562		⌐	
700		⌐	
437	G		
436	▨		
434		⌐	
433		⌐	
310		⌐	

Stitch Count: 31 x 26

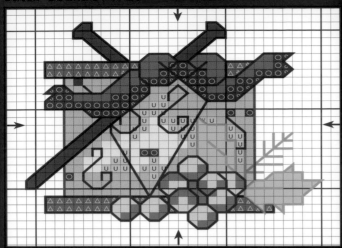

Stitch Count: 29 x 31

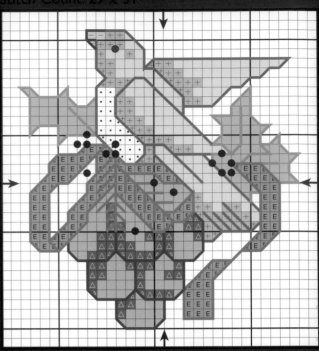

Stitch Count: 34 x 41

DMC Floss			
	XS	BS	FK
White	·		
745			
744	—		
676			
948			
351			
350	⊙		
666	■	⌐	
816		⌐	
3747			
340			
333		⌐	
775			
3325	+		
798		⌐	
806	▫		
563			
562		⌐	
989	E		
702			
700	N	⌐	
739			
437	U		
436			
435	△		
433	■	⌐	•
310		⌐	•

Stitch Count: 34 x 26

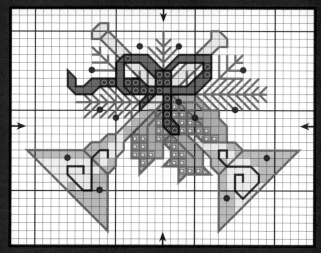

Stitch Count: 37 x 32

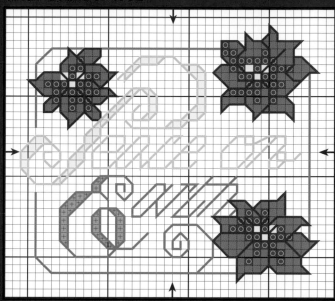

Stitch Count: 26 x 12

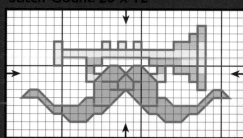

DMC Floss				DMC Floss		
	XS	BS	FK		XS	BS
677				333		⌐
676				913		
351				563		
350	⊙			562	⊡	⌐
666		⌐	●	700		⌐
340				434		⌐

Stitch Count: 77 x 13

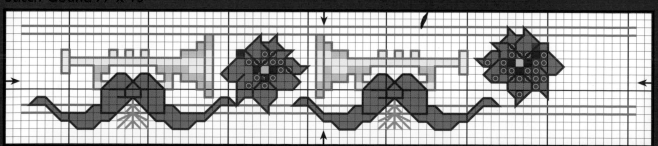

Merry Christmas Sampler

Stitched On: White Aida 14 over 1
Finished Design Size: 12" x 16¾"
Cut Fabric: 18" x 23"
Stitch Count: 168 x 225

Stitch Count: 24 x 27

Code for pages 82–85.

DMC Floss	XS	BS	FK	DMC Floss	XS	HC	BS	FK
White	·			809	★		⌐	
745	☐			792	■		⌐	●
744	+			704	☐			
676	△			702	◎			
729	M	⌐		3817	☐			
3770	◣			954	⊡	/		
948	☐			912	✳			
3733	■			911	■		⌐	●
3705	N			561	♥		⌐	●
608	■	⌐		3827	☐			
606	⊡			402	✕			
666	■	⌐	●	976	■			
304	E	⌐	●	435	☐		⌐	
815	■	⌐		841	☐			
775	☐			840	S			
827	⊡			839	■		⌐	●
826	■		●	318	K			
824	☐	⌐		414	■			
996	H			310	■		⌐	●

Code for pages 86–87.

DMC Floss	XS	BS	FK	DMC Floss	XS	BS	FK	DMC Floss	XS	BS	FK
White	·			800	☐			739	−		
746	☐			813	⊡			738	☐		
744	◎			3766	△			976		⌐	
676	☐			312		⌐		435	■		
729	B			772	☐			434		⌐	
776			●	912	■			801		⌐	
3609	✕			911	★		●	452	☐		
350	◪			909	◻			451	✳		
666	+	⌐		3816	E			413		⌐	●
321	■	⌐	●	3818		⌐		310	■	⌐	●
304		⌐		561	H	⌐					

Stitch Count: 22 x 34

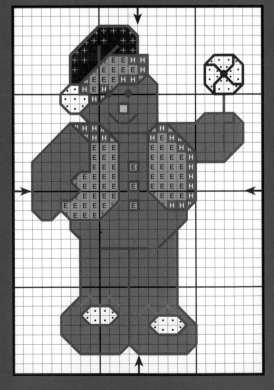

Stitch Count: 21 x 43

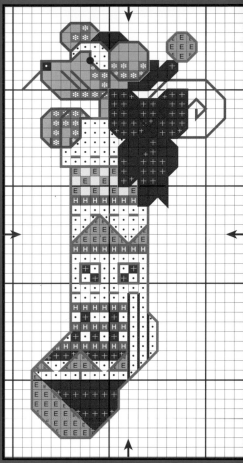

Stitch Count: 24 x 37

Stitch Count: 27 x 26

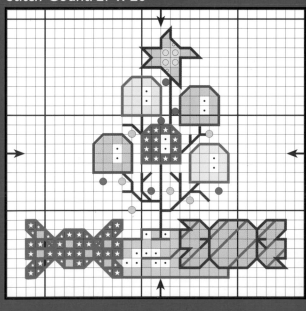

Stitch Count: 28 x 27

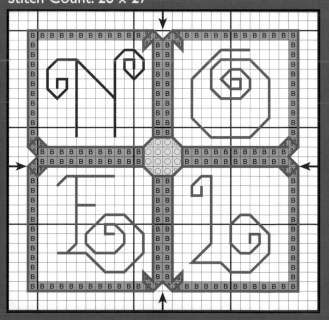

Stitch Count: 25 x 57

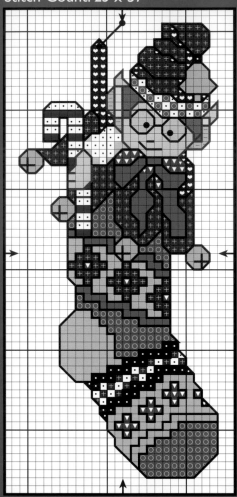

Stitch Count: 36 x 43

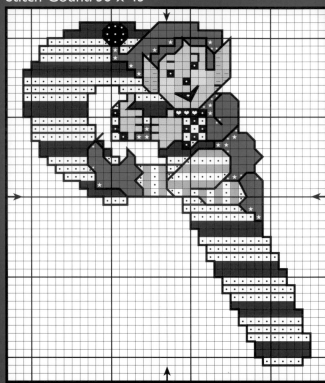

Stitch Count: 16 x 43

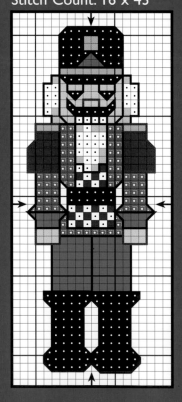

DMC Floss			DMC Floss			
	XS	BS		XS	BS	FK
White	⋅		907			
972			911			
818			909	★		
666	■	⌐	3345	◎		
321	+		738			
815	♥	⌐	436	=		
3753			434			
798			801		⌐	
797	▼		310	■	⌐	●
824	⋅					

Stitch Count: 34 x 29

Our
First
Christmas
Jason & Robin
1900

Stitch Count: 39 x 40

Stitch Count: 30 x 27

DMC Floss			
	XS	BS	FK
White	·		
3821		⌐	
3770			
758		·	
605		·	
603			
602		⌐	
666		⌐	●
3753			
931	H		
312			
911			
909		⌐	●
3772		⌐	
842			
841	E	⌐	
938		⌐	
310	·	⌐	●

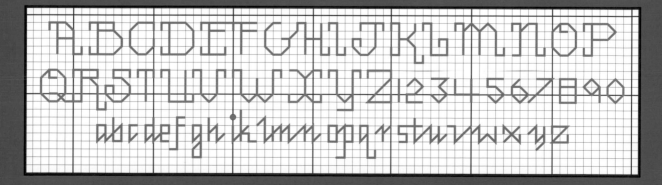

Stitch Count: 20 x 44

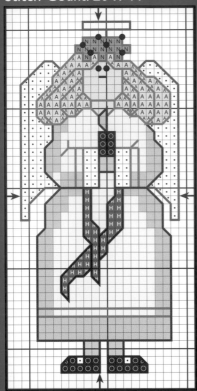

Stitch Count: 35 x 26

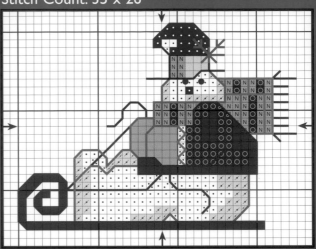

Stitch Count: 37 x 33

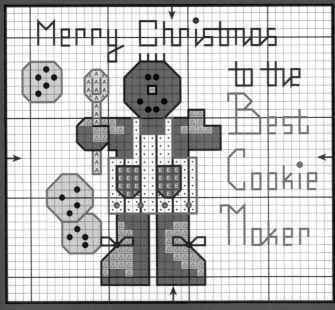

DMC Floss			
	XS	**BS**	**FK**
White	·		
746	□		
745	A		
676	▦		
948	▢		
776	▬		
666	■	⌐	●
321	◉	⌐	●
304		⌐	
775	◹		
813	▦		
793	E		
312		⌐	
909		⌐	●
561	H		
3817	▦		
3816	N		
3818		⌐	
976		⌐	
738	▦		
436	△		
435	▦		
434		⌐	
801		⌐	
898	■		●
310	▣	⌐	●

Stitch Count: 35 x 38

Stitch Count: 15 x 41

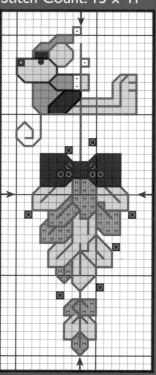

Stitch Count: 35 x 43

DMC Floss			DMC Floss				
	XS	BS		XS	BS	FK	LS
White	·		907				
972			3347	⁙			
818			3345	⁝			╲
352			3817				
666			3816	H			
321	⊙		3818				
304		⌐	738	−	⌐		
815	▣		436				
798			434				
824	Z	⌐	801	⁙	⌐		
312		⌐	453				
912			413		⌐		
911	E		310	·	⌐	●	

91

Stitch Count: 27 x 24

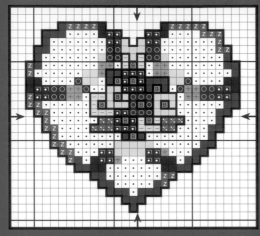

Stitch Count: 25 x 31

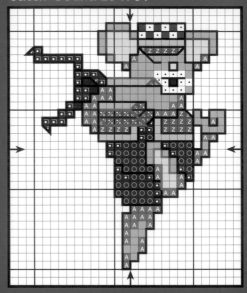

Stitch Count: 25 x 34

Stitch Count: 46 x 26

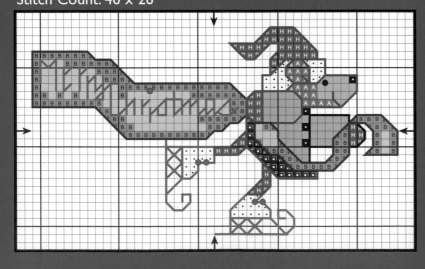

DMC Floss			
	XS	**BS**	**FK**
White	·		
745	−		
676			
729	B		
818			
352	+		
350			
666	◉		
321	▣		
815	■	⌐	
210			
799			
797			
824	Z	⌐	●
907			
3345	▨		
913	✕		
911			
561	H	⌐	●
435			
801		⌐	
415			
414	A		
413		⌐	
310	▣	⌐	●

Stitch Count: 68 x 72

DMC Floss			DMC Floss		DMC Floss		
	XS	BS		XS		XS	BS
White	·		775	▨	701		⌐
776	▨		702	▧	310	▪	⌐
666	■	⌐					

Stitch Count: 30 x 43

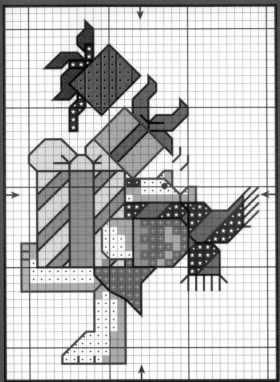

Stitch Count: 24 x 45

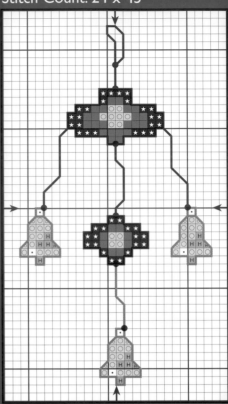

Stitch Count: 34 x 43

DMC Floss	XS	BS	DMC Floss	XS	BS	FK
White	·		3325	▨		
745	▨		798	▨		
444	–		797	▼		
972	▨		796		⌐	
3822	◎		793	+		
3820	H		913	▨		
729	▨		911	▪		
3829		⌐	910	▨		
351	▨		909	✳	⌐	
350	▨		738	▨		
666	★	⌐	436	E		
321	▨		434	▨		
304		⌐	801	N	⌐	
815	♥		415	▨		
209	▨		310	▪	⌐	●

94

Stitch Count: 32 x 55

Stitch Count: 20 x 27

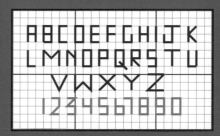

Stitch Count: 43 x 30

DMC Floss			
	XS	**BS**	**FK**
White	⊡		
745			
743	+		
972			
776			
350	▨		
666	■		●
321	◉		
815	■	⌐	●
800			
798		⌐	
702			
911			
909	▣	⌐	●
738			
436	△		
434			
801	■	⌐	●
414	A		
317		⌐	
310	⊡	⌐	

Stitch Count: 36 x 36

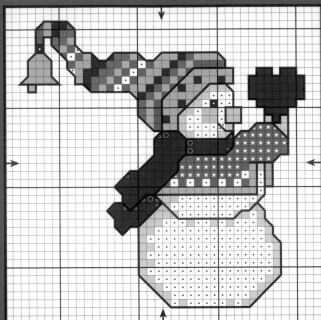

Stitch Count: 30 x 36

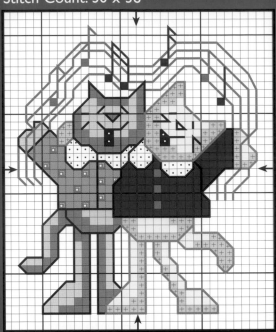

Stitch Count: 52 x 38

DMC Floss			
	XS	BS	FK
White	·		
677			
676	+		
729			
972			
776			
350			
666		⌐	●
321			
816	◎	⌐	
209			
3753			
794			
793	▫	⌐	
824			
772			
913			
911	★		
909		⌐	●
738			
434		⌐	
453			
452	H		
451			
310	▪	⌐	●

Stitch Count: 52 x 27

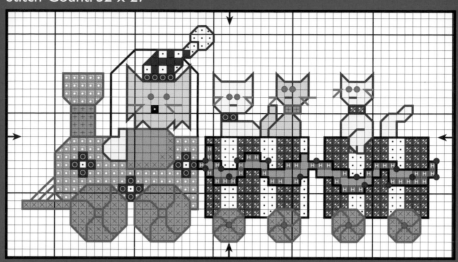

Stitch Count: 37 x 51

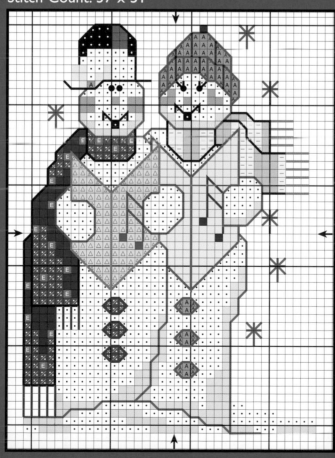

DMC Floss			
	XS	BS	FK
White	·		
746	▢		
744	△		
677	−		
676	▨		
3716	▨		
350	▣		
666	■	⌐	
321	◉		●
304		⌐	
775	▢		
813	▨		
826	✕		
793	E		
798		⌐	
312		⌐	●
772	▢		
989	A		
3816	▨		
913	▣		
912	+		
699	■	⌐	
561	H		
738	▨		
435		⌐	
801		⌐	
451	▨	⌐	●
310	▣	⌐	●

Stitch Count: 42 x 41

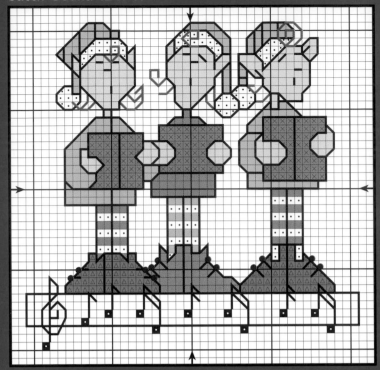

Stitch Count: 46 x 10

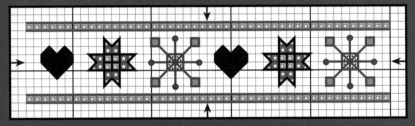

Stitch Count: 48 x 29

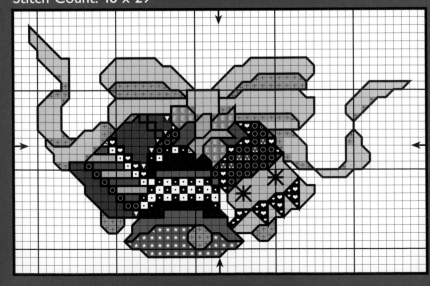

DMC Floss			
	XS	**BS**	**FK**
White	⊡		
444			
972	+		
948			
3326			
666	■	⌐	●
321	◉		
304		⌐	
815	♥		
3753			
813			
794	✕		
798	■		
797	▼		
824	⬚		
312		⌐	●
955			
913	⊡		
911			
909	★		
907			
3347	E		
3345			
562	▲		
3818		⌐	
434		⌐	
801		⌐	
310	■	⌐	

Stitch Count: 29 x 45

Stitch Count: 28 x 35

Stitch Count: 46 x 21

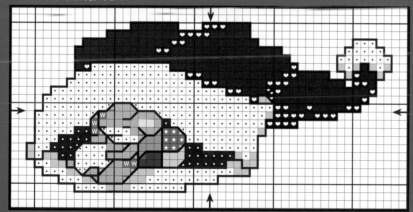

DMC Floss			
	XS	BS	FK
White	·		
444			
972	⊠		
948			
352			
350			
666	⊡		
321			
815	♥		
3753			
3325	⊞		
794			
793	▣		
797			
796		⌐	
702			
700		⌐	
909	★		
738			
436	H		
434			
801		⌐	
415			
414	w		
310	▪		●

Stitch Count: 37 x 34

Stitch Count: 25 x 44

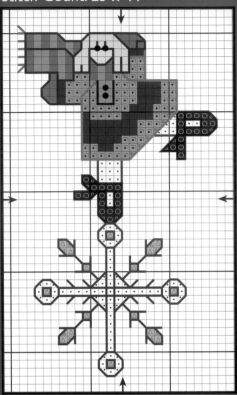

Stitch Count: 41 x 39

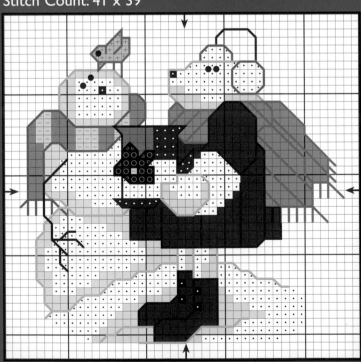

DMC Floss			
	XS	BS	FK
White	·		
745			
744	−		
676	+		
729			
948			
350	■	⌐	
666	◉	⌐	
321	E	⌐	
815	■	⌐	
341			
340		⌐	
775			
3325	▲	⌐	
702			
700		⌐	
913	▣		
911			
909	★	⌐	
738	▨		
436			
434		⌐	
801	N	⌐	
451			
310	▪	⌐	●

Stitch Count: 55 x 34

DMC Floss			DMC Floss				DMC Floss			
	XS	BS		XS	BS	FK		XS	BS	FK
White	·		775				700	■	⌐	●
745			3325	△	⌐		699		⌐	
743	−		794	+			434		⌐	
351	■		793	■			453			
350	⊙		796		⌐	●	452	H		
666	■	⌐	704				451		⌐	
815	E	⌐	702	·			310	·	⌐	●

Stitch Count: 54 x 29

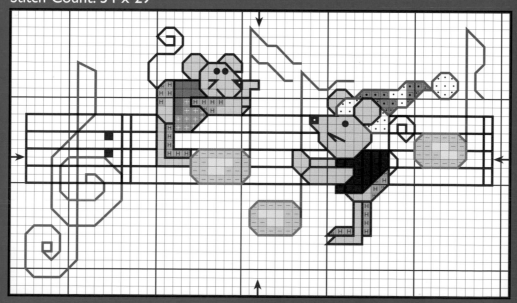

Stitch Count: 56 x 22

Stitch Count: 25 x 23

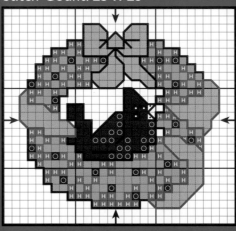

Stitch Count: 39 x 26

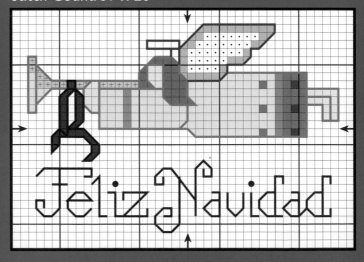

DMC Floss			
	XS	**BS**	**FK**
White	⊡		
745			
676	⊞		
948			
350	■		
666	◉		
321	■		
304		⌐	●
210			
3325			
793	■		
796		⌐	
702			
700	▣		
699		⌐	
3816			
562			
561	E		
435	■		
434		⌐	
452			
413		⌐	
310	▪	⌐	●

Stitch Count: 17 x 24

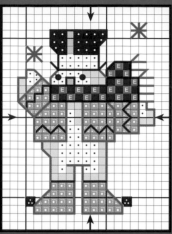

DMC Floss				DMC Floss			DMC Floss			
	XS	BS	FK		XS	BS		XS	BS	FK
White	·			321	▣		913	▣		
745	−			304		⌐	911	E		
743				775			3818		⌐	
677				3325		⌐	436			
676	N			312		⌐	435			
776				793			434		⌐	
351				564			453			
350	◎	⌐		563	+		310	▣	⌐	●
666	■	⌐	●	562						

Stitch Count: 60 x 66

Nature
Christmas

on thee shine
nd Joy be always thine

Nature Christmas Sampler

Stitched on: Ivory Aida 14 over 1
Finished Design Size: 12" x 16"
Cut Fabric: 16" x 22"
Stitch Count: 168 x 224

Code for pages 106–109.

DMC Floss	XS	HC	BS	FK	LS
White	·			○	
3078	▫				
676	▪				
742	▨			●	
351	▪				
666	■			●	
321	✳		⌐		
3756	▫				
775	◎				
799	N				
797	■		⌐		
931		╱			
704⟩ 772	▫				
703	▪				
911	▪				
699	E		⌐		╱
3817	▫				
3816	▪				

DMC Floss	XS	BS	FK	LS
3827	▪			
977	⊞	⌐		
976	■			
3776	★			
920	■			
739	☑			
738	△			
436	z			
434	▪			
842	▪			
841	u			
840	⊡			
839	■	⌐		╱
3024	▪			
647	▪			
645	♥	⌐		
310	▪	⌐	●	

Code for pages 110–111.

DMC Floss	XS	BS	FK
White	·		
727	▫		
729	▪		
352	▪		
350	◪		
666	A	⌐	
321	■		
816	⊡	⌐	●
3722	★		
209	▪		
552		⌐	
799	▪		
797	■	⌐	●
966	▫		
320	⊞		
3347	▪	⌐	
3345	■	⌐	
909	◎		
738	▫		
437	⊠		
436	B		
435	E		
434	▪	⌐	
801		⌐	

Stitch Count: 31 x 41

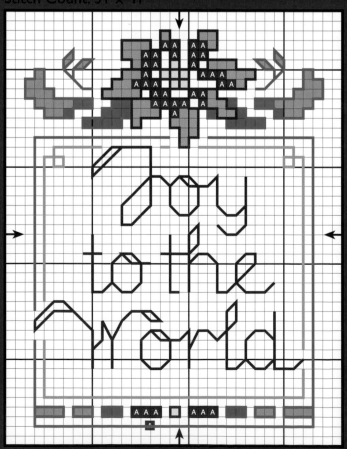

Stitch Count: 32 x 22

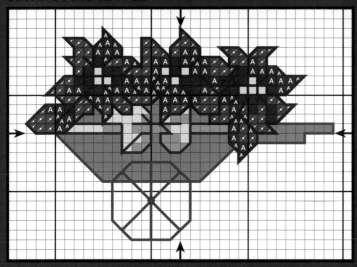

Stitch Count: 30 x 20

Stitch Count: 29 x 15

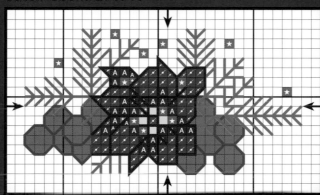

Stitch Count: 53 x 32

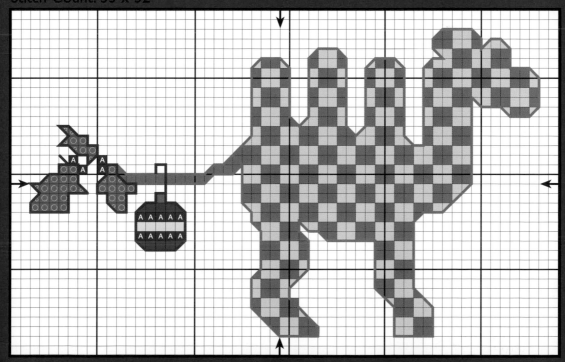

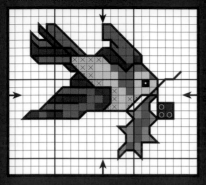

Stitch Count: 20 x 17

Stitch Count: 39 x 36

DMC Floss			DMC Floss			
	XS	BS		XS	BS	FK
White	⊡		3345	■		
444	▨		738	▨		
972	✚	⌐	436	⊠		
666	■		434	▨		
321	◎		801	■	⌐	
815	■		415	▨		
3753	▨		414	E	⌐	
798	■		317		⌐	
824	z		310	⊡	⌐	●
3347	▨					

Stitch Count: 50 x 51

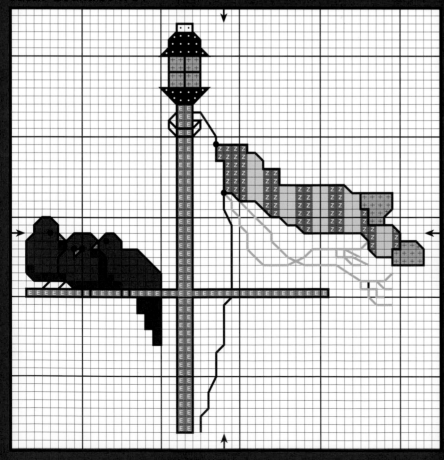

Stitch Count: 17 x 51

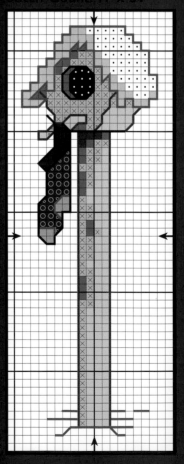

Stitch Count: 26 x 20

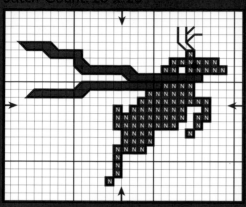

Stitch Count: 40 x 21

Stitch Count: 40 x 29

DMC Floss				DMC Floss			
	XS	BS	FK		XS	BS	FK
White	⊙			3347	▦		
712	▢			3345	▣	⌐	
444	⊞			907	E		
725	▨		●	909	▦		
972	▢	⌐		500		⌐	●
818	▢			920		⌐	
352	◉			738	▢		
606	△			436	⊟		
666	■			434	▦		
321	⊠	⌐		801	N	⌐	
815	■			310	⊡	⌐	●
3348	▨						

Stitch Count: 34 x 41

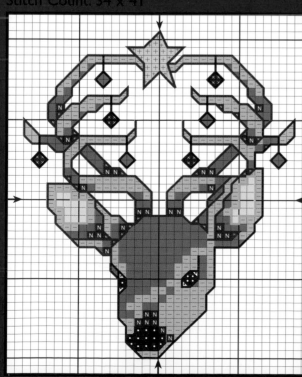

Stitch Count: 31 x 38

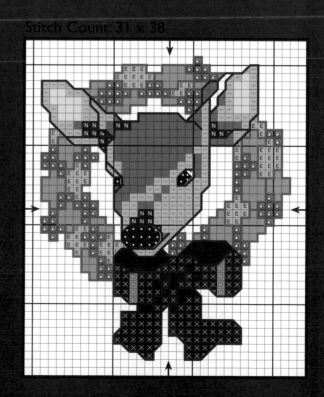

115

Stitch Count: 31 x 22

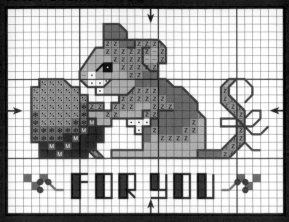

FOR YOU

Stitch Count: 40 x 37

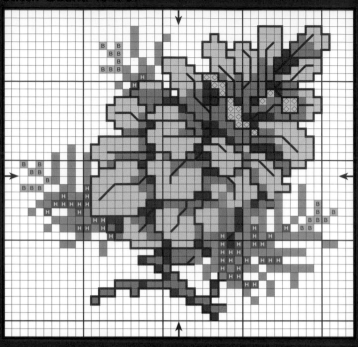

Stitch Count: 33 x 30

and Heaven and Nature Sing

Stitch Count: 40 x 36

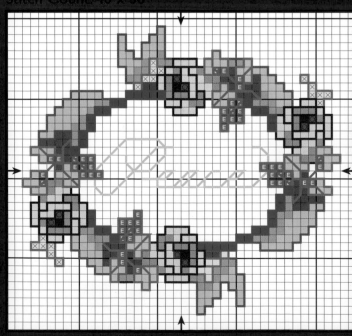

DMC Floss				DMC Floss			
	XS	BS	FK		XS	BS	FK
White	·			3346	■	⌐	
725	■	⌐		3345	H		
3774	■			402	⚬		
606	■	⌐	●	977	■		
818	■			922	✳		
776	−			921	■	⌐	
3326	■			738	◇		
335	◉			3033	■		
326	■	⌐		842	Z		
800		⌐		841	■		
772	⊠			840	M		
472	B			839	■	⌐	
368	■			938		⌐	
367	E	⌐		762	■		
319	■	⌐		452	△		
3348	+			310	▣	⌐	●
3347	■						

Stitch Count: 24 x 26

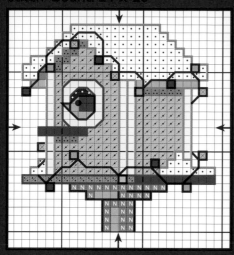

Stitch Count: 34 x 25

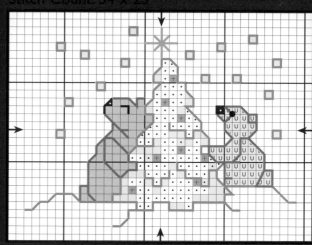

Stitch Count: 28 x 24

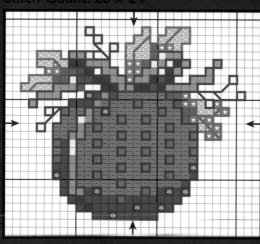

DMC Floss			DMC Floss				DMC Floss			
	XS	BS		XS	BS	FK		XS	BS	FK
White	·		666	■			3345	■	⌐	
746	□		321	◉			950	■		
725	■		3350	■	⌐		3064	⊘		
3820	+	⌐	816	■	⌐	●	407	■		
722	■		3756	□			632	■	⌐	
720	■		813	■			739	U		
977	■		334	■	⌐		437	■		
352	△		369	□			434	■	⌐	
921	●	⌐	472	⊠			840	■		
606	■		3053	E			839	✳	⌐	
776	⊿		3051	■			801	■	⌐	
3716	■		3348	◇			415	■		
899	⊡	⌐	3347	H			414	M	⌐	
961	■		3346	★			310	⊡	⌐	●

Stitch Count: 28 x 24

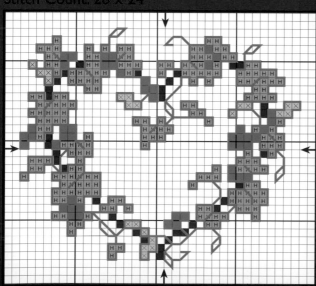

Stitch Count: 39 x 39

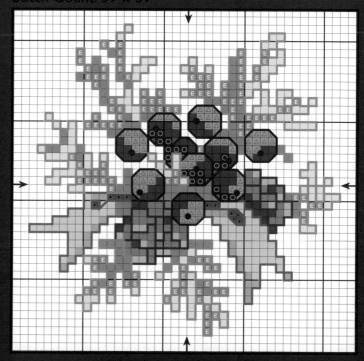

115

Stitch Count: 69 x 18

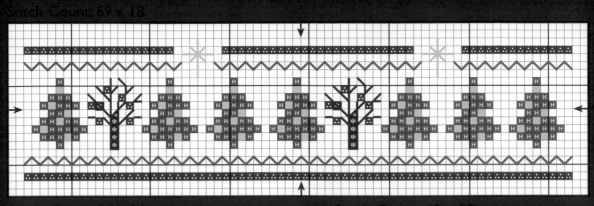

Stitch Count: 34 x 36

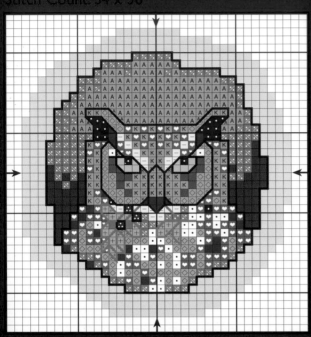

Stitch Count: 40 x 37

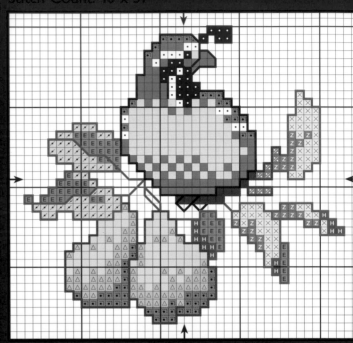

Stitch Count: 40 x 37

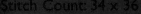

DMC Floss				DMC Floss			DMC Floss	
	XS	BS	FK		XS	BS		XS	BS
White	·			470	▪	⌐	632	✦	⌐
746	−			3348	▨		543	□	
745	□		○	3347	E		842	A	
677	☒			3346	▪		841	▨	
725	□			3345	H	⌐	839	▪	⌐
606	▪			437	△		801	❋	⌐
666	▪			922	▪		762	□	
321	◉	⌐		921		⌐	415	K	
815	▪	⌐		920			318	▪	
772	□			977	▪		451	♥	
3053	Z			402	◇		535	▪	⌐
472	+			3064	▪		310	▪	⌐

Stitch Count: 40 x 38

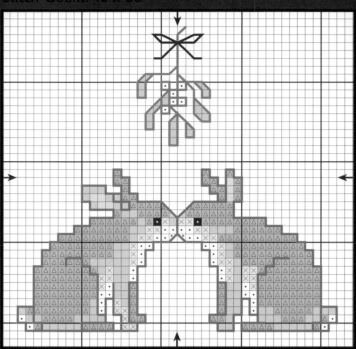

Stitch Count: 22 x 21

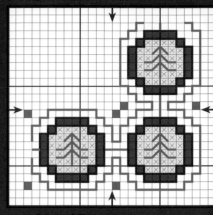

Stitch Count: 30 x 37

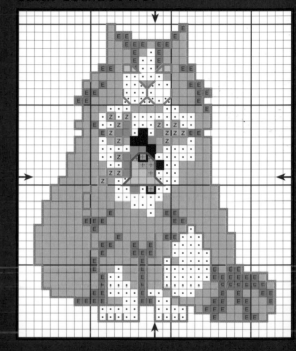

DMC Floss			DMC Floss			DMC Floss			DMC Floss			
	XS	BS		XS	BS		XS	BS		XS	BS	FK
White	·		321	▨		3347			436	◺		
746	□		816	■	⌐	3345	◎	⌐	434			
725			798	■	⌐	561	■		400	■		
818			704	z		977	+		415			
3326	A		702		⌐	402			414	N	⌐	
899			368			921	■	⌐	318	E		
606	■	⌐	367		⌐	799	⋈		310	■	⌐	●
666		⌐	3348	▭		738						

Stitch Count: 38 x 38

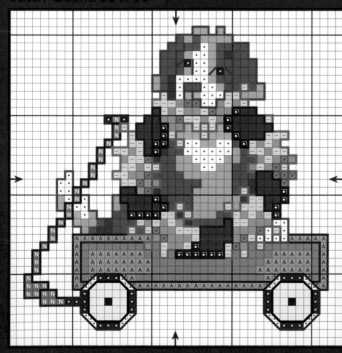

Stitch Count: 31 x 32

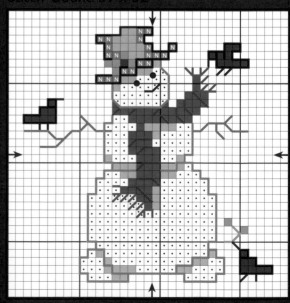

Stitch Count: 28 x 25

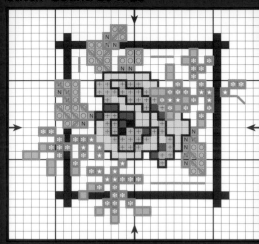

Stitch Count: 29 x 25

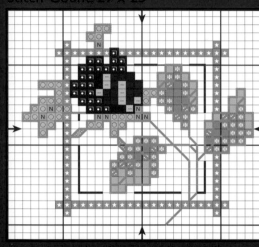

Stitch Count: 40 x 38

Stitch Count: 40 x 40

Stitch Count: 30 x 30

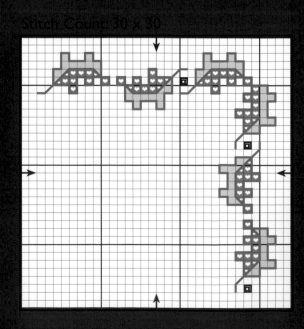

DMC Floss			DMC Floss			DMC Floss		
	XS	BS		XS	BS		XS	BS
White	·		321	▣		937	★	
727			816	■	⌐	3348	✕	
3341	–		554	■		3347	⊡	
352			209	△	⌐	3345	■	
606	■		3013			368		
818			3012	✳		367	♥	
776	+		3011		⌐	319	■	⌐
335	■		472	◎		977		
666	■	∟	471	N		921	E	⌐

Stitch Count: 19 x 19

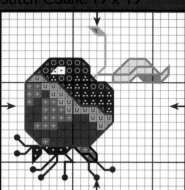

Stitch Count: 24 x 21

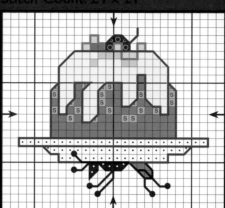

Stitch Count: 24 x 27

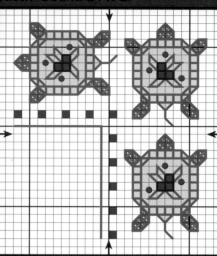

Stitch Count: 33 x 33

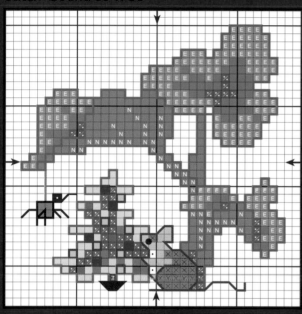

Stitch Count: 38 x 16

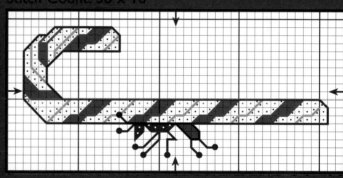

Stitch Count: 36 x 37

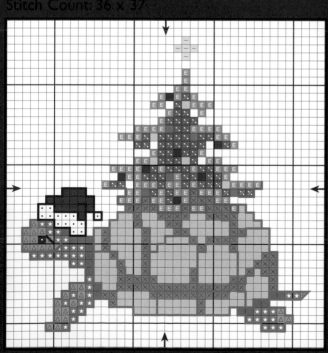

DMC Floss				DMC Floss			
	XS	BS	FK		XS	BS	FK
White	·			3348			
746				3347	E	⌐	
727	—			3346		⌐	
725				3345	⊠	⌐	
606	■	⌐	●	738			
970	■			950	S		
776				407	■		
666	◉	⌐		3773	U		
321	⊡			3772	+		
816	■	⌐		632	■		
209	■			3033			
800				841	⊠		
3053	■			840		⌐	
3052	N			839	Z	⌐	
471	△			414	■	⌐	
470	★			310	⊡	⌐	●
469	■	⌐					

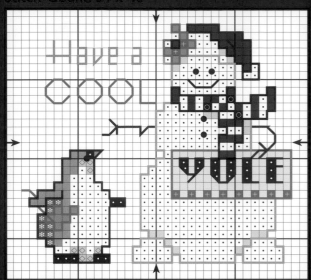

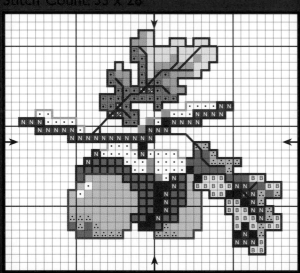

DMC Floss			DMC Floss			DMC Floss		DMC Floss			
	XS	BS		XS	BS		XS		XS	BS	FK
White	·		817	◎		920	▨	433	N		
712	B		912			402		801			
744			909	+		739		647			
948			472			738	◇	645	✳		
722	△		471	E		437	∴	844			
720			470	★		436		3072			
352	✕		469			434		310	■		●
350			922								

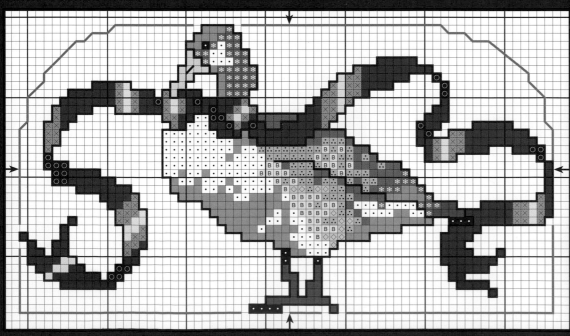

Stitch Count: 38 x 40

Stitch Count: 34 x 49

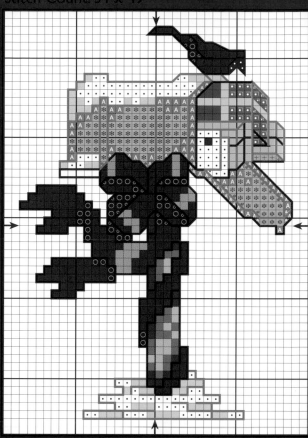

Stitch Count: 39 x 39

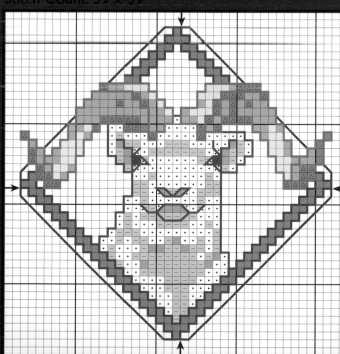

DMC Floss			DMC Floss		
	XS	BS		XS	BS
White	·		841	◣	
712	B		840	■	⌐
444	▦		739	□	
972	+		738	◇	
948	▫		436	▦	
606		⌐	435	▣	
776	×		434	▦	
352	▦		433	E	⌐
321	■	⌐	801	■	
815	◉	⌐	453	—	
3753	▨		452	▦	
799	▦		762	□	
798	▣		415	✳	
797	▦	⌐	414	A	
907	▦		317		⌐
402	H		413	■	⌐
842	▦		310	▪	⌐

Stitch Count: 40 x 39

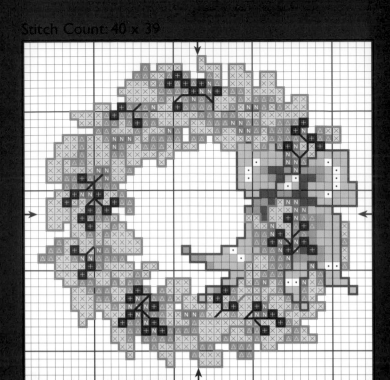

Stitch Count: 26 x 41

DMC Floss		DMC Floss			DMC Floss			DMC Floss			DMC Floss		
XS			**XS**	**BS**		**XS**	**BS**		**XS**	**BS**		**XS**	**BS**
White	·	899	◎		503	◪		3051	H		833	✳	⌐
677	▫	3705	◼		502	◼	⌐	3348	☒		921	◼	
725	▪	309		⌐	472	▪		3347	△		920	◼	⌐
977	▪	326	◼		471	z		3346	N	⌐	3064	▪	
606	+	321	E	⌐	3053	◙		3345	◼	⌐	632	◼	⌐
776	▪	504	▫		3052	◼							

Stitch Count: 37 x 40

Stitch Count: 34 x 40

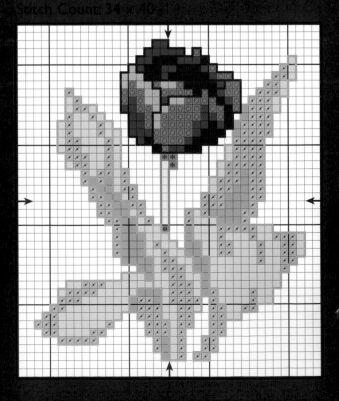

Stitch Count: 22 x 22

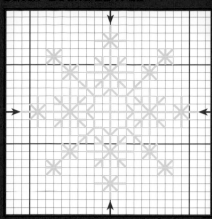

Stitch Count: 39 x 34

Stitch Count: 29 x 21

Stitch Count: 21 x 23

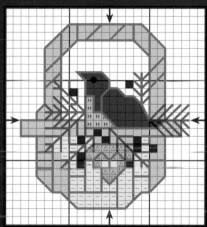

Stitch Count: 39 x 39

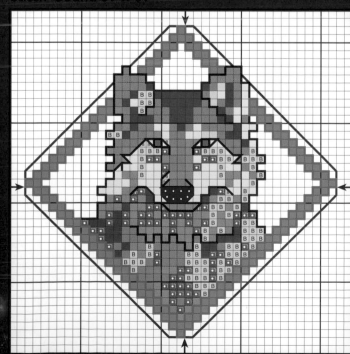

DMC Floss				DMC Floss			
	XS	BS	FK		XS	BS	FK
White	·			3346	■		
712	▫			3345		⌐	
676	H			739	‒		
3047	B			437	▫		
3045	■			436	△		
948	▫			435	■		
606	+	⌐		434		⌐	
350	■			3022	■		
600	■			869	▫		
816		⌐		842	▫		
333	■			841	N		
775	◪			839	■		
800		⌐		415	▫		
312		⌐		414	E	⌐	
703	▫			535	■		
701	◉	⌐	●	310	▪	⌐	●
699		⌐					

123

Stitch Count: 38 x 33

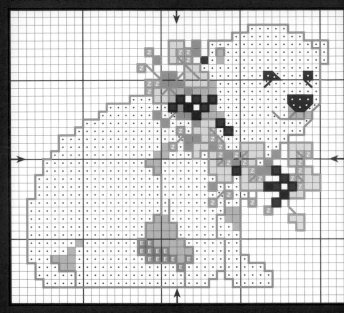

DMC Floss				DMC Floss			
	XS	BS	FK		XS	BS	FK
White	·			3347	■	⌐	
677	▫			504	▫		
676	+			502	Z		
606	■			501	■		
3731	■			702	■	⌐	
350	■			699	■	⌐	
666			●	841	▫		
321	■	⌐		739	◿		
3350		⌐		437	▫		
816		⌐		436	▣		
3747	−			434		⌐	
333	■	⌐		433	■	⌐	
775	▫			415	▫		
796		⌐		318	E		
369	▫			535	■		
368	△			310	■	⌐	●
472	⊠						

Stitch Count: 77 x 16

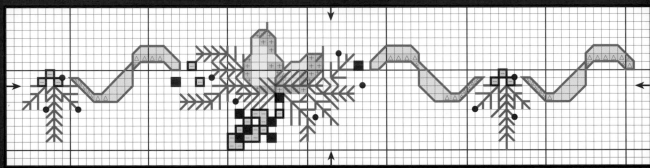

Stitch Count: 33 x 35

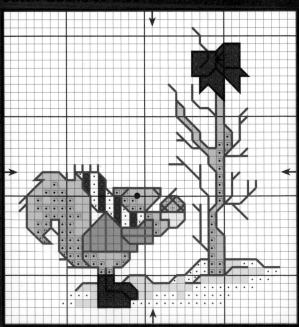

Stitch Count: 39 x 39

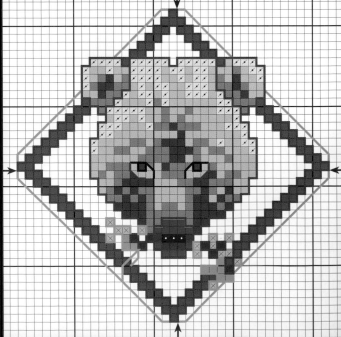

Stitch Count: 40 x 39

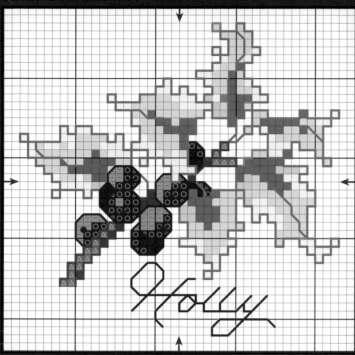

Stitch Count: 28 x 28

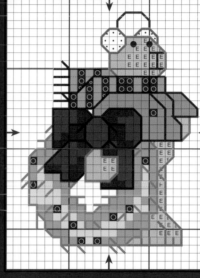

Stitch Count: 22 x 30

DMC Floss				DMC Floss			DMC Floss		
	XS	BS	FK		XS	BS		XS	BS	FK
White	·			312		⌐	839	■	⌐
746	□			3348			738		
744				3347	+		437	E	
352	–			3345		⌐	436		
350	■			966			435	■	
776		·		912			434	H	
666	◉			911	◙		801		⌐
321	■	⌐	●	561		⌐	453		
800				842			451	■	
807				840	△		310	▪	⌐	●
826	✕								

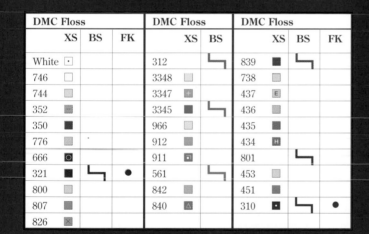

Stitch Count: 26 x 33

Stitch Count: 40 x 31

125

Anchor Conversion Chart

DMC	Anchor	DMC	Anchor	DMC	Anchor	DMC	Anchor	DMC	Anchor
B5200	1	368	214	561	212	727	293	815	44
White	2	369	1043	562	210	729	890	816	43
Ecru	387	370	888	563	208	730	845	817	13
208	110	371	887	564	206	731	281	818	23
209	109	372	887	580	924	732	281	819	271
210	108	400	351	581	281	733	280	820	134
211	342	402	1047	597	1064	734	279	822	390
221	897	407	914	598	1062	738	361	823	152
223	895	413	236	600	59	739	366	824	164
224	893	414	235	601	63	740	316	825	162
225	1026	415	398	602	57	741	304	826	161
300	352	420	374	603	62	742	303	827	160
301	1049	422	372	604	55	743	302	828	9159
304	19	433	358	605	1094	744	301	829	906
307	289	434	310	606	334	745	300	830	277
309	42	435	365	608	330	746	275	831	277
310	403	436	363	610	889	747	158	832	907
311	148	437	362	611	898	754	1012	833	874
312	979	444	291	612	832	758	9575	834	874
315	1019	445	288	613	831	760	1022	838	1088
316	1017	451	233	632	936	761	1021	839	1086
317	400	452	232	640	393	762	234	840	1084
318	235	453	231	642	392	772	259	841	1082
319	1044	469	267	644	391	775	128	842	1080
320	215	470	266	645	273	776	24	844	1041
321	47	471	265	646	8581	778	968	869	375
322	978	472	253	647	1040	780	309	890	218
326	59	498	1005	648	900	781	308	891	35
327	101	500	683	666	46	782	308	892	33
333	119	501	878	676	891	783	307	893	27
334	977	502	877	677	361	791	178	894	26
335	40	503	876	680	901	792	941	895	1044
336	150	504	206	699	923	793	176	898	380
340	118	517	162	700	228	794	175	899	38
341	117	518	1039	701	227	796	133	900	333
347	1025	519	1038	702	226	797	132	902	897
349	13	520	862	703	238	798	146	904	258
350	11	522	860	704	256	799	145	905	257
351	10	523	859	712	926	800	144	906	256
352	9	524	858	718	88	801	359	907	255
353	8	535	401	720	325	806	169	909	923
355	1014	543	933	721	324	807	168	910	230
356	1013	550	101	722	323	809	130	911	205
367	216	552	99	725	305	813	161	912	209
		553	98	726	295	814	45	913	204
		554	95						

915	1029	986	246	3607	87	3799	236	**Variegated Colors**	
917	89	987	244	3608	86	3801	1098		
918	341	988	243	3609	85	3802	1019	48	1207
919	340	989	242	3685	1028	3803	69	51	1220
920	1004	991	1076	3687	68	3804	63	52	1209
921	1003	992	1072	3688	75	3805	62	53	——
922	1003	993	1070	3689	49	3806	62	57	1203
924	851	995	410	3705	35	3807	122	61	1218
926	850	996	433	3706	33	3808	1068	62	1201
927	849	3011	856	3708	31	3809	1066	67	1212
928	274	3012	855	3712	1023	3810	1066	69	1218
930	1035	3013	853	3713	1020	3811	1060	75	1206
931	1034	3021	905	3716	25	3812	188	90	1217
932	1033	3022	8581	3721	896	3813	875	91	1211
934	862	3023	899	3722	1027	3814	1074	92	1215
935	861	3024	388	3726	1018	3815	877	93	1210
936	846	3031	905	3727	1016	3816	876	94	1216
937	268	3032	898	3731	76	3817	875	95	1209
938	381	3033	387	3733	75	3818	923	99	1204
939	152	3041	871	3740	872	3819	278	101	1213
943	189	3042	870	3743	869	3820	306	102	1209
945	881	3045	888	3746	1030	3821	305	103	1210
946	332	3046	887	3747	120	3822	295	104	1217
947	330	3047	852	3750	1036	3823	386	105	1218
948	1011	3051	845	3752	1032	3824	8	106	1203
950	4146	3052	844	3753	1031	3825	323	107	1203
951	1010	3053	843	3755	140	3826	1049	108	1220
954	203	3064	883	3756	1037	3827	311	111	1218
955	203	3072	397	3760	162	3828	373	112	1201
956	40	3078	292	3761	928	3829	901	113	1210
957	50	3325	129	3765	170	3830	5975	114	1213
958	187	3326	36	3766	167			115	1206
959	186	3328	1024	3768	779			121	1210
961	76	3340	329	3770	1009			122	1215
962	75	3341	328	3772	1007			123	——
963	23	3345	268	3773	1008			124	1210
964	185	3346	267	3774	778			125	1213
966	240	3347	266	3776	1048			126	1209
970	925	3348	264	3777	1015				
971	316	3350	77	3778	1013				
972	298	3354	74	3779	868				
973	290	3362	263	3781	1050				
975	357	3363	262	3782	388				
976	1001	3364	261	3787	904				
977	1002	3371	382	3790	904				

Metric Conversion Chart

mm-millimetres   cm-centimetres
inches to millimetres and centimetres

inches	mm	cm	inches	cm	inches	cm
1/8	3	0.3	9	22.9	30	76.2
1/4	6	0.6	10	25.4	31	78.7
3/8	10	1.0	11	27.9	32	81.3
1/2	13	1.3	12	30.5	33	83.8
5/8	16	1.6	13	33.0	34	86.4
3/4	19	1.9	14	35.6	35	88.9
7/8	22	2.2	15	38.1	36	91.4
1	25	2.5	16	40.6	37	94.0
1 1/4	32	3.2	17	43.2	38	96.5
1 1/2	38	3.8	18	45.7	39	99.1
1 3/4	44	4.4	19	48.3	40	101.6
2	51	5.1	20	50.8	41	104.1
2 1/2	64	6.4	21	53.3	42	106.7
3	76	7.6	22	55.9	43	109.2
3 1/2	89	8.9	23	58.4	44	111.8
4	102	10.2	24	61.0	45	114.3
4 1/2	114	11.4	25	63.5	46	116.8
5	127	12.7	26	66.0	47	119.4
6	152	15.2	27	68.6	48	121.9
7	178	17.8	28	71.1	49	124.5
8	203	20.3	29	73.7	50	127.0

Index